Structuring Your Organization for Innovation

Structuring Your Organization for Innovation

Jane Keathley, MS
H. James Harrington, PhD

Quality Press
Milwaukee, Wisconsin

American Society for Quality, Quality Press, Milwaukee, 53203.
© 2020 by Jane Keathley, MS and H. James Harrington, PhD.
All rights reserved. Published 2020.
Printed in the United States of America.

25 24 23 LS 5 4 3 2

Publisher's Cataloging-in-Publication Data

Names: Keathley, Jane, author. | Harrington, H. James, author.
Title: Structuring your organization for innovation / Jane Keathley, MS ;
H. James Harrington, PhD.
Description: Includes bibliographical references and index. | Milwaukee, WI:
Quality Press, 2020.
Identifiers: LCCN: 2020948256 | ISBN: 978-1-951058-29-6 (pbk.) |
978-1-951058-30-2 (epub) | 978-1-951058-31-9 (pdf)
Subjects: LCSH Business. | Success in business. | Creative ability in business.
| Management. | Industrial organization. | Industrial management. |
BISAC BUSINESS & ECONOMICS / Decision-Making & Problem Solving |
BUSINESS & ECONOMICS / Organizational Development
Classification: LCC HD53 .K426 2020 | DDC 650.1 – dc23

ASQ advances individual, organizational, and community excellence
worldwide through learning, quality improvement, and knowledge exchange.

Bookstores, wholesalers, schools, libraries, businesses, and organizations:
Quality Press books are available at quantity discounts for bulk purchases
for business, trade, or educational uses. For more information, please contact
Quality Press at 800-248-1946 or books@asq.org.

To place orders or browse the selection of all Quality Press titles, visit our
website at: http://www.asq.org/quality-press.

Quality Press
600 N. Plankinton Ave.
Milwaukee, WI 53203-2914
Email: books@asq.org

ASQ Excellence Through Quality™

I dedicate this book to Owen and Sadie,
whose curiosity and creativity inspire me.

— Jane D. Keathley

I dedicate this book to Chuck Mignosa and
Neal Kuhn in appreciation of their friendship and
willingness to help me improve my quality of life.

— H. James Harrington

Table of Contents

Acknowledgments

I GREATLY APPRECIATE Dr. Harrington's invitation to collaborate on this book and to gain insights into his extensive knowledge of innovation and quality. Many others have personally helped advance my knowledge of innovation and organizational structure, and I am grateful for their insights. Included among them are Peter Merrill, Nicole Radziwill, Therese Steiner, and Carolyn Maki. ASQ's Body of Knowledge and online resources were very helpful in researching aspects of the book. My husband Jim patiently supported me throughout the book's development.

– Jane D. Keathley

IT IS HARD FOR ME TO DEFINE just one person — or even two, three, or four people — who have helped mold my thinking so it is in line with the information contained in this book. Chuck Mignosa, Neal Kuhn, my son James Harrington, Doug Nelson, Jane Keathley, and Frank Voehl have all contributed unselfishly of their knowledge, background, and experience.

– H. James Harrington

Foreword

INNOVATION, INNOVATION, INNOVATION—that's all you hear anymore. Everything is innovative, if you listen to people on TV or talk with salespeople about any new products. You will be informed that your new telephone is innovative, that new car is innovative, that hair shampoo is innovative, the baby's diapers are innovative, the new pencil set is innovative, the oil painting I did in my spare time is innovative, the new Thermos jug is innovative, I am innovative because I'm wearing a blue shirt instead of my normal white shirt, etc. (A person from the International Organization for Standardization (ISO) committee on innovation stated that "innovation" was anything an individual did differently than he or she had done previously. Using that as a definition, changing my toothpaste from one brand to another is innovative. I think not!) No matter where you go or what you do, someone is putting the innovation label on it.

Has the focus shifted from quality to innovation? Today's customers are naturally interested in products and services that reflect the latest and greatest technologies, for example, the latest feature updates for smartphones and watches, or the flashy new electric car. That initial enthusiasm may quickly fade, however, if the quality and performance of that new technology doesn't deliver as promised. The quality of the product or service remains critically important to the organization's success.

This does not diminish the role innovation has come to play in successful performance. Staying ahead of customers' expectations and competitors' offerings, as well as addressing the never-ending supply of major problems, challenges, and opportunities facing us all, has made it clear that organizations must be able to respond nimbly, creatively, and, well, innovatively if they wish to remain viable. Indeed, chief executives cite concerns about digital disruption, hiring the right (i.e., creative and innovative) talent, and maintaining a culture of innovation among their biggest challenges.

We used to think of R&D staff as the only people with a passport to innovation. As we learned with quality, innovation is everyone's responsibility. It is a mindset and part of the organization's culture. Just as with quality, innovation must be developed and sustained through leadership, policies, recognition, and measures.

A key element of an organization's culture lies in its structure. The organization's structure is a system that defines the hierarchical reporting lines within the organization, its functional arrangements, and, at a high level, its operations. The structure describes communication channels, decision pathways, where work gets done, and interfaces among and between groups. Structuring an organization can play a significant role in the organization's ability to innovate effectively, and it is this element of innovation that we will explore in this book.

Given that innovation practices build on and utilize many quality practices, our discussion of structuring for innovation will be made through the lens of quality. Innovation management is considered by some people to be at a similar maturation point as quality management was in the 1960s. The lessons that were learned as quality management came of age over the past few decades have applicability in the rapidly advancing age of innovation. Among those lessons learned are how various organizational models contribute (or don't contribute) to quality. Structuring an organization to improve quality outcomes can also improve innovation outcomes. It is with these thoughts in mind that we prepared this book.

CHAPTER ONE

Organizational Structure Design

YOU MAY HAVE HEARD the following story before — it is an excellent example of how organizational structures can be misused.

The Johnson Tool and Die Company had seen a steady loss of customers for the last four years. Wages had continued to go up due to the lack of availability of experienced, trained tool makers. At the same time, the product sales price had dropped due to cheaper labor costs in Asian countries. The stockholders had not received a dividend in the last three years, and reserve funds were almost depleted. An emergency meeting was held of the board of directors, and the decision was made to replace the present chief executive officer (CEO), John Smith. Smith agreed to stay on for four additional weeks to provide overlap with the incoming CEO, Pat McManaman.

At 8:00 p.m. on the last day of John's employment at the Johnson Tool and Die Company, after all the goodbyes had been exchanged between John and his former employees, John walked to his car in the parking lot. Pat intercepted him there and broke the silence by saying, "Is there any last-minute advice you can give me that will help me be successful in replacing you?"

John explained, "The CEO job is a lonesome job. The employees are unhappy with you because they want to be paid more. The board is unhappy with you because the dividends are too low and stock prices have not increased as much as they would like. The customer is unhappy with you for too many reasons to mention now. I want you to succeed, as I have dedicated eight years of my life to this company. To help you in your new job, I have prepared three envelopes. Without being too creative, each one is marked with a number. A year from now when everyone is complaining because this situation has not improved, open the envelope marked '1.'"

John's prediction held true, so Pat proceeded to open envelope 1 after his first year as CEO. It was a short memo saying, "Blame the lack of progress on the previous management team. This will give you a little time to really turn things around. If after year two everyone is still unhappy with you, open envelope 2."

Another year slipped by, and things had not improved. In fact, the condition had gotten worse. The workers were threatening to go on strike if they didn't get a 10% raise across the board. The stock market was down 24%, but the stock's value had decreased only 18%. It was time to open envelope 2. The one-page memo in this envelope read, "Blame the lack of progress on the organizational structure and reorganize the company. If people are still unhappy with your progress, open envelope 3."

Following John's advice, Pat restructured the organization, dividing up the smokestack type of functions, making them part of each of the product lines. Everyone saw this as a major change, and, obviously, Pat was going to make a difference in the organization's performance.

In almost the blink of the eye, 18 months passed by with little or no progress in generating increased revenue so the workers could get a pay increase and the quarterly dividend could be increased. It was time to open envelope 3. Inside the envelope, there was a sheet of paper with just one sentence on it. It read, "Write three memos."

Now, we shared this long story just to prove the point that reorganization is not just moving some names around on the organization chart. Every reorganization, no matter how small or how big, creates significant stress on the total organization. Every time the organization's structure is modified, a complete business-case analysis should be performed to ensure the added stress is offset by significantly added value for the organization, i.e., value added for employees, a reasonable return on investment, and increased customer satisfaction. All too often reorganizational structure is based on one or two individuals who want to increase their power and their perception of prestige.

For years management has looked at reorganization as the magic wand that can solve all the problems. The truth is, it really is an illusion that can hide the true nature of the problems.

IBM provides an excellent example of the reorganization syndrome. Back in the early 1980s, John Akers became president of IBM. At that time, IBM owned the mainframe and personal computer (PC) markets. The decision was made to focus on the mainframe market where the margins were much higher than those in the PC market. This decision reflected the inputs they received from many of their major customers that were, at the time, disappointed with the way PCs were being used. Comments like, "The PC is turning our PhDs into secretaries and greatly reducing the time they have to do creative/innovative work."

By the mid-1980s, it became obvious that IBM had misjudged the PC market, as it was growing faster than the mainframe requirements. IBM's profits, stock values, and prestige suffered greatly from this mistaken premise. To help bring costs under control, IBM encouraged its workers to retire by providing them with more incentives if they retired right away. As a result, many of their best and brightest employees, who could easily find new jobs in the fast-developing IT market, left the company. All too often, the employees who remained were the least innovative and creative IBM employees, as they would have had difficulty finding other employment at the same level of pay.

To offset this negative trend, IBM restructured parts of the organization, appointing John Akers as president and chairman of the board. Of course, this primarily eliminated many of the checks and balances that a board of directors would normally exercise. To offset these negative trends, John Akers reorganized IBM numerous times until many of the stockholders were so disappointed that they threatened to replace the board of directors if something was not done. This threat led to a mass resignation, including John Akers and a number of the executive management team.

From our point of view, John Akers' mistake was that he tried to reorganize IBM to turn it around; we believe that what he needed to do was to change the priorities within the organization: "The company's weakness is the inflexibility of its management structure."

INNOVATION—TODAY'S NECESSITY

"We might as well require a man to wear the coat which fitted as a boy."

– Thomas Jefferson, third President of the United States

When Thomas Jefferson made this statement, he was discussing the need to reorganize the way governments were structured. His thoughts are still true to both the public and private sectors. As our organizations grow, we can let out the structural seams just so much before we need to alter the structure for a better fit. In these cases, a holistic approach is required. This chapter discusses the things that should be considered and how to go about making an assessment that results in a successfully redesigned organizational structure.

The structure of an organization refers to the formal way in which people and work are grouped. Any organization with more than two dozen people or so will need to begin to group them together to manage the work effectively. Grouping activities and positions into organizational units establishes common focus through shared objectives, processes, and access to information, and a common model for decision-making. It can enhance the efficient use of organizational resources and provides employees with an identifiable "home" within the larger organization.

The structure sets out the basic power relationships in the organization — how limited resources such as people and funds are allocated and coordinated. The structure defines which organizational components and roles are most central for execution of the strategy and how the business's profit centers are configured.

No one structure is best for every organization. The best structure is the one that helps the organization achieve its strategy. There are multiple ways to structure the organization to achieve its goals. As with any design choice, each involves trade-offs and compromises. The objective in choosing a structure is to maximize as many of the strategic design criteria as possible, while minimizing negative impacts.

ORGANIZATIONAL STRUCTURE DESIGN PERSPECTIVES

As you consider your organization's structure and whether changes need to be made to it, the question becomes, "What is the best organizational fit for my strategy and competitive environment and makes best use of my distinct core competencies?" The answer to this comes not from a single diagnostic tool but, rather, from a technique of "informed dialogue," which is a combination of analysis and discussion conducted in an interactive way.

What is the best way to decide on the "right" structure and fit for an organization? The first step in this process is to look at the organization from three perspectives: strategic, operational, and tactical. These three perspectives comprise what is called organizational structure. It is the combination of strategic, operational, and tactical decisions that will be the basis for determining the "right" organizational structure, and, if done well, it can drive a structure that is highly successful at innovation.

Strategic Perspective

The strategic perspective looks at the organization from the top down and determines its overall shape. It is a process of moving the big boxes around to determine the right fit and how to best allocate and focus resources to carry out the strategy of the organization. To start this process, develop an understanding of the current state of the organization and its environment. Some questions to explore are:

- How does the competitive environment shape the way we conduct business? Is a specific structure forced on us by competitors?

- How well do we meet our customers' demands? How does structure affect our ability to meet customers' demands?

- What are the interrelationships among the different functions and units, and how do they impact each other? How can the structure support coordination among them?

- What are our core competencies? How well do they support our strategy? How can structure facilitate the strategy?

- What impacts do our history and culture have on how we have structured our organization? What barriers could they impose on a new structure?

The answers to these questions will have a dramatic impact on what you can and should do with your structure. For example, if reacting to a volatile market where customer needs are constantly changing is the number one strategic issue, then a decentralized product design unit attached to a horizontally based organization makes more sense than a centralized design center at corporate headquarters. (In Chapter 2, we explore the various types of organizational structures in greater detail.)

To focus the effort of answering these questions, consider developing a structure vision matrix looking at data input, influencing principles, and output options. Table 1.1 illustrates how one organization used this approach. The structure vision matrix is normally conducted over a period of weeks where information is first collected on the data inputs, which is then presented and filtered through the influencing principles with the resultant outputs used to help set the direction for the next step, which is to address the operational perspective.

Data inputs	Principles	Output options
Market trends		
Customer needs		
Competitors	Level management	Vertical
Business performance	Customer oriented	Matrix
Suppliers	Growth vs. cost	Network
Industry trends	Employee involvement	Case management
History	Process orientation	Horizontal
Strategic plan	Market oriented	Process management
Organizational values		
Employee skills		

Table 1.1 Example of an organizational structure visioning matrix.

Not all structured visions need to be so complete and formal. One organization simply developed some bullet points:

- Manage by process rather than function.

- Achieve a common goal of satisfying the customer.

- Have departments interact with each other before making policy or procedures changes.

- Lessen finger-pointing between departments and divisions.

- Give employees a chance to understand their own functions (job responsibilities) in respect to the entire system.

- Provide consistency in work between departments (i.e., every individual performing the same task in a similar manner).

- Help employees learn from each other.

To encourage more innovative, forward thinking, the goals of the organizational structure should be to achieve better coordination among functions, decentralize authority, increase employee involvement at lower levels of the organization, restructure the decision-making process, and more clearly define roles and responsibilities. The predominant need is for a cross-functional focus, reducing the isolation of functions among divisions. A structure for innovation most likely will require features of a horizontal organization where structure is built around processes and teams. These cross-functional teams will be focused on the four basic processes (financial, product development, production, and sales and marketing) and a flatter organization to drive decision-making authority to a lower level.

Operational Perspective

The next step is to review the design impact of the strategic perspective and establish how the organization can cluster its work to support the strategic intent and direction of the business. The operational perspective deals with the strategic business units. In this case, you look at the organization from two directions. Review the strategic fit with a look from the top down. Ensure the appropriate mix of operational, managerial, and support processes through a bottom-up review.

One approach is to use three grouping options. These are activity, output, and segment (see Table 1.2). Each grouping has relative advantages and disadvantages in terms of competitive response, market response, and internal functioning and strategy implementation.

Grouping option	Structural implications	Example
Activity • Function • Knowledge/skill	All personnel who contribute to or accomplish similar activities or who perform similar functions are grouped together.	Auto manufacturers have historically used activity as the primary method of grouping; i.e., marketing, manufacturing, and service were all separate divisions.
Output • Product • Service • Project	All specialists needed to produce a given product, service, or project work together.	Contract research organizations generally operate in a project-based environment where cross-functional teams are assembled to deliver the required clinical research expertise for the project.
Segment • Market/industrial • Users/clients • Geography	All specialists needed to serve an industrial/market segment, meet user/client needs, or serve distinct territories work together.	Banking typically is divided by region, with some divisions serving the east, central, and western portion of the country.

Table 1.2 Analysis of three operational grouping options.

Dividing the organization by activity is similar to the traditional vertical organization where activity is defined as a function or knowledge group. Such an organization would have predominantly functional components at the highest level, such as finance, operations, sales and marketing, etc. Divisions based on activity usually promote high functional expertise and utilize staff efficiently. This is particularly effective where functional expertise and knowledge transfer are key to a strategy. However, since the work process tends to run across divisions, interdivisional tensions are likely to be observed.

Dividing the organization along output lines allows each product group to focus on the efficient production of a specific product/service. Such an organization would have predominantly product/service components at the highest level, such as consumer electronics, industrial products, warranty operators and components, etc. Divisions based on product/service usually promote increased product innovation and productivity advantages. They tend to provide a rapid response to existing markets. This is highly effective in a competitive market where production efficiencies are key. On the other hand, coordination of marketing activities across different product groups is generally less effective. Also, any leverage that may be achieved with supplier and distribution channels through coordinated purchasing and logistics is generally less than that of activity designs.

Dividing the organization along segment lines allows each group to focus on the responsive delivery of products and services. Segments may be divided by geographic industrial/market segment or user/client needs. This method results in specific structures like the Americas group, European operations, high-net-worth clients, etc. Divisions based on segment typically promote faster time to market or enhanced customer sensitivity and focus. They tend to have well-integrated customer support systems and rapid response to customer needs. It is highly conducive to a market in which customized products or services are the norm.

Most organizations use two or all of these groupings. For example, within traditional, activity-grouped organizations where the largest divisions are operations, sales, and service, subdivisions may be based on output or segment. The key is being able to identify the right combination. Most of the answers for this will come from the strategic perspective process and the development of the structural vision. Remember that the operational perspective is the bridge between the strategy of the organization and the tactical way in which the work is performed. It is important to keep in mind that the groupings are not mutually exclusive of each other. In fact, the most effective organization uses all types of groupings. They may be grouped by activities at the senior management level, by market segment at the division level, by product output at the plant management level, and by user segment at the work flow or process level.

Tactical Perspective

Finally, the tactical perspective is completed with a bottom-up approach and determines the work team and job designs. Tactical design plays a big part in determining the basis for the right organizational structure that enhances innovation. Whether we are dealing with a team of people or an individual, we still need to determine how to structure work at a tactical level in ways that allow creativity, agility, and focus. As with the previous two perspectives, there are some questions to ask, and the answers will give us direction in this process.

1. To what degree does the job have a clearly identifiable beginning and produce a meaningful product or service? What is the interval of time between completing a task and the completion of the work process?

2. What categories of work logically are grouped together for an individual or team? What is the relationship each task has with the task preceding and following it?

3. How should work be managed and coordinated? Who makes the decisions? What level of decision-making is made? How should decisions be made?

4. How do information and knowledge flow? Is feedback complete, immediate, direct, and individualized on tasks and operational completeness?

5. How routine is the work? Is it governed by standard methods and procedures? Does it change from day to day, or customer to customer?

It is the cumulative knowledge of the three structural perspectives—strategic, operational, and tactical—that finally provides you with the data necessary to put together a design plan for the organizational structure. But, just in case you feel that is the end of the process, there is still one more organizational frontier to address.

IMPLEMENTATION AND POTENTIAL BARRIERS

Once the strategy is set, the design is established, and the work plan is in place, you are ready to begin implementation.

Some changes may be of such magnitude that it will take a Herculean effort on the part of management. For example, a successful movement from hierarchical, functional behavior to a team-based organization requires patience and long-term commitment, tolerance for error, and behavioral role models. The transition process can be measured in years, not months, and unless the organization is committed to this investment, the transition may fail, and management is likely to lose credibility with its employees.

Dr. H. James Harrington points out, "A major restructuring change in any organization should only be undertaken when it will produce a very significant performance improvement, and then it must be accompanied with an effective organizational change management plan."

There are numerous inherent barriers to the successful implementation of structural changes: senior management preferences, organizational culture, regulatory issues, and current customers' demands. These barriers can usually be divided into two types: organizational and transitional. For instance, if you were going to change from a traditional vertical organization to a team-based horizontal organization, you might encounter the following organizational barriers:

- **Management/Leadership development needs**

  Reduction of levels of management will result in increased levels of accountability for managers. Successful implementation will require careful assessment of readiness of managers to take on additional responsibility. Senior management, which has carried out much of the day-to-day business decision-making, needs to be ready to relinquish much of this authority to the business team level, and needs to have patience in the development of the team members to take on such responsibility.

- **Functional walls**

  For horizontal teams to work, the members need to shift some of their identity to the team and away from their functional area. The history of functional focus in the culture may present some tension in starting up teams. When functional organizations look to improve, they normally focus on improvements within their own functions.

- **Team leadership**

  Horizontal process teams need to have an owner who understands the complete process across all functions and has credibility to sponsor and sustain implementation.

Transitional barriers to structural changes should also be expected and addressed. They may be associated with friction or resistance during the transition.

- **Friction**

  Friction barriers are passive and a direct result of the change itself. Disruptions of work, communications, decision-making, and organizational power are direct consequences of the transition efforts. Although this kind of change should not directly halt the progress of the structural transition, it can slow things down, and if left unchecked, it can create an environment where active resistance will occur.

- **Resistance**

  Resistance barriers represent active resistance to the transition process. An example of this is the backlash that occurs as a result of increased organizational friction. Should the change process become too disruptive, active resistance to the change itself may emerge.

Understanding and anticipating the barriers to the transition to a new structure helps to determine how to get to your desired future state and should be included in the change management or project plan. Remember, structural transitions are evolutionary and are similar to a learning-curve process, wherein each advancement represents the refinement of the previous stage. In the early stages of development, it is helpful for experts to be involved in chartering teams, establishing objectives, defining processes, and monitoring performance. As the organization and its employees gain experience and new skills, the transitional activities can be successfully incorporated into the operating levels of the organization.

ORGANIZATIONAL STRUCTURE DESIGN PHASES

Although there are many different processes that can be used to develop a customized innovative organizational structure, the following four phases capture the key elements.

Phase I: Determining the design framework (strategy)

Input: Current-state assessment

Output: The organizational capabilities that are needed to fulfill the strategy

Phase II: Designing the organization (operations)

Input: Design framework

Outputs:

- Structure—instructional and organizational design with goals that are in line with the strategy
- The process and lateral capabilities—how work will be coordinated and integrated across business units
- Reward systems—how performance will be measured and rewarded at the individual, team, and organization level
- People—how people will be selected and deployed into new roles, their performance managed, and their development supported

Phase III: Developing the details (tactical)

Input: Organizational design

Output: Updated change management project plan defining how the pieces will work together

Phase IV: Implementing the new design

Input: Change management plan for the transition project

Output: Project completed and the affected resources moved into the transition state

CHAPTER TWO

Different Types of Organizational Structure

DR. H. JAMES HARRINGTON STATES, "As much as I would like to tell you that everyone should evolve to a network organization, I cannot. My experience indicates that multiple types of organizational structures and even combinations of them must be considered depending on the organization environment."

Deciding what organizational structure to establish can be highly subjective. Understanding how to design and deploy an organizational structure that results in the desired level of innovation and performance will benefit from knowledge of the various types of structures commonly in use. Transitioning from one model to a different one may be what is needed; blending more than one model or customizing a model (perhaps the one you already have) are other possible approaches. The descriptions of the various types of models in this chapter will help you determine which model to pursue. They are listed here and summarized in Table 2.1.

The most commonly used organizational structures:

- Functional
  - Vertical
  - Bureaucratic

- Decentralized
  - Geographic
  - Product
  - Customer
  - Front-back hybrid

- Matrix

- Network
  - Case management system
  - Horizontal process management network

Option	Advantages	Disadvantages
1. Functional *Organized around major activity groups such as R&D, operations, finance, or HR*	• Increases knowledge sharing within functions • Eliminates costly duplication, allowing maximum specialization in trained occupational skills because of the individual grouping specialties • Provides leverage with vendors • Offers economies of scale • Allows for standardization of processes and procedures	• Is difficult to manage diverse product and service lines • May have contention and delays in decision-making caused by cross-functional processes • May fail to develop well-rounded top managers, especially when higher-level management makes the decisions
2. Vertical *Organized around functions with centralized corporate staff directing labor and production*	• Clearly defines scope of tasks • Requires a limited range of knowledge or skills to perform effectively • Enhances knowledge transfer along the chain-of-command • Enhances competency development within a vertical unit • Provides efficiency in stable, predictable environments	• Offers limited flexibility or exposure to other responsibility areas • Offers limited career development opportunities • Is difficult to transfer knowledge across the organization • Provides a narrow skills base within a vertical unit • Is ineffective in dynamic or unpredictable environments
3. Bureaucratic *Organized around functions with complex and multilayered management structures*	• Provides well-defined policies and procedures, roles, and responsibilities • Stables organization systems and processes • Provides consistent service and quality levels	• Has potential for long cycle times when process crosses many responsibility areas • Provides glacial responsiveness to change • Offers no individual judgment or empowerment • Tends to have performance expectations that are internally focused

Table 2.1 Overview of the different organizational structures' advantages and disadvantages. *(continued)*

Option	Advantages	Disadvantages
4. Decentralized *Organized around independent business units with authority over its operations and results*	• Enables business units to be more responsive to changes in customer needs, market demands, and their respective external environments • Empowers business units to focus competency development efforts in areas that support their own success • Empowers business units to develop their own standards within corporate guidelines • Provides accountability and control at the business unit level • Offers less managerial overhead, greater opportunity for manager development as decision-making is delegated	• Is difficult for entire enterprise to act in concert • Is hard to coordinate business units when a customer is in multiple segments • Provides duplication of resources and inefficiency at an enterprise level • Presents difficulty transferring knowledge across business units • Has high potential for inconsistent processes, technologies applications, and competence levels • May cause internal tension and competition for resources
5. Geographic *Organized around physical locations such as states, countries, or regions*	• Provides a local focus • Moves decision-making authority closer to the situation • Permits accountability for performance • Provides mechanisms for the organization to react quickly, such as to competitive changes or new customer needs	• Can be difficult to mobilize and share resources across regional boundaries • Duplicates costly resources (i.e., equipment and personnel) between departments • Encourages competition among divisions • Reduces specialization in occupational skills • Is less advantageous with technology advances

Table 2.1 Overview of the different organizational structures' advantages and disadvantages. *(continued)*

Option	Advantages	Disadvantages
6. Product *Organized into product divisions, each with its own functional structure to support product lines*	• Provides more rapid product development cycles • Allows for state-of-the-art research focus • Puts P&L responsibility for each product at the division level with a general manager • Develops positive team spirit around products	• May have divergence among product lines in focus and standards • May make it hard to recognize when a product should be changed or dropped because of loyalty to product division • Spreads out functions, causing lost economies of scale • Offers multiple points of contract for the customer
7. Customer *Organized around major market segments such as client groups, industries, or population groups*	• Provides the ability to customize deliverables for customers, including mass customization • Provides the ability to build depth in customer relationships • Offers greater ability to provide packaged solutions	• Presents divergence among customer/market segments in focus and standards • Duplicates resources and functions • Spreads out functions among customer/market divisions, causing lost economies of scale
8. Front-back hybrid *Combines elements of both the product and customer structures in order to provide the benefits of both*	• Allows customers to buy multiple products with a single point of contact and one account • Enables organizations to better cross-sell their products • Offers the ability to provide value-added systems and solutions when products have become commodities • Preserves product focus and product excellence • Allows for a variety of distribution channels	• Causes contention over where resources are allocated • Causes disagreements over prices and customer needs • Is difficult to coordinate marketing functions that are split between the front and the back • Presents conflicting metrics • Makes information sharing and accounting complex

Table 2.1 Overview of the different organizational structures' advantages and disadvantages. *(continued)*

Option	Advantages	Disadvantages
9. Matrix *Functional groups (e.g., product or customer) are superimposed on a functional structure*	• Allows greater customer focus while retaining functional integrity • Works best in a complex and dynamic environment • Is effective in project-based industries	• Increases organizational tension and confusion from dual reporting structures • May drive conflict over resource assignments • Requires balance or sharing of power among managers
10. Network *Organized around teams of people working on a common goal (e.g., process or client)*	• Is aligned strategically • Is customer focused • Provides total accountability for process performance • Aligns workforce along process lines • Makes all resources to do the job available within the network • Lowers process cycle time • Executes processes efficiently	• Duplicates resources • Presents competing goals across process teams and across levels of hierarchy • Causes stressful work environment due to high levels of interdependence • Creates complex career pathing and potential to create glass ceiling • Reduces critical mass or economies of scale • Dissipates knowledge
11. Case management network *Organized around cross-functional teams of people working on a common case (e.g., patient)*	• Offers total accountability for customer satisfaction • Provides job diversity • Eases coordination between functions • Is highly decentralized and cross-functional • Is responsive to customer needs and market requirements	• Presents the potential for variability and inefficiencies in the delivery of products and/or services • May cause stressful work environment due to high levels of interdependence • Requires highly skilled employees • Presents unclear roles and responsibilities • Reduces enterprise focus

Table 2.1 Overview of the different organizational structures' advantages and disadvantages.   *(continued)*

Option	Advantages	Disadvantages
12. Horizontal process management network *Organized around core processes (e.g., order fulfillment and the requirements needed to meet customer needs for that process)*	• Flattens organizational hierarchy • Links performance objectives to customer satisfaction • Provides job diversity and skill development • Increases supplier and customer contact • Is responsive to both customer and internal needs • Provides opportunities for individuals and for teams	• Typically requires blend of vertical and horizontal features • May cause stressful work environment due to high levels of interdependence • Requires highly skilled employees with multiple competencies • Requires roles and responsibilities to be clearly assigned

Table 2.1 Overview of the different organizational structures' advantages and disadvantages.

FUNCTIONAL STRUCTURE

A functional structure is organized around major activity groups such as operations, R&D, marketing, finance, and human resources (HR). The functional structure is best for companies that:

- Have a single line of business

- Are small and/or have a stable environment

- Require common standards

- Have a core capability that requires depth of expertise in one or more functional areas

- Do not have a diverse line of products

- Do not compete in the marketplace based on speed of product development cycle times

An example of a company that uses a functional structure is Amazon.com (Meyer 2019a; Dudovsky 2018). Amazon bills itself as providing "Earth's Biggest Selection." Through its marketplace e-commerce platform, it offers books, videos, music, toys, home improvement products and electronics, beauty products, sporting goods, groceries, pet supplies, jewelry, and almost anything else. In addition, other vendors can sell their products through the marketplace for a fee, providing them access to Amazon's huge customer base. Amazon gains another revenue stream and also widens its range of offerings without taking on inventory management and costs. Amazon has set the standard in online product selection, searching, and ease of ordering, as well as an easy-to-use payment interface that automatically recalls the customer's preferred shipping address and payment method. It partners with shipping businesses for order delivery.

Amazon's strategy is to be both customer-centric and operationally excellent. It wants to create a place where customers can find anything they want in one place and count on superior customer service. By carefully choosing the companies with which it partners and through its online product reviews, Amazon has positioned itself as an advocate for the consumer. The message conveyed is, "We're giving you as much information as we can so you can make the best choice."

Amazon's goal—"to get big fast"—has been criticized by those who note that it failed to turn a profit in its first six years after its initial public offering and subsequently bounced between low or no profits for the next 12 years (Griswold and Karaian 2018). However, rapid growth allowed Amazon to gain a competitive edge by creating communities of users who come to Amazon to find others with similar interests and for Amazon to collect information on these customers and engage in highly customized marketing. The bet is that by offering customers more than just selection and easy ordering, they are less likely to go elsewhere. This innovative business model is paying off for Amazon, which has been highly profitable for the past several years.

Although Amazon sells many products, it does not produce any, and its primary line of business is to provide access to those products through e-commerce. As a retail operation, Amazon's structure needs to provide IT, operations, customer service, and logistics capabilities along with the flexibility to continually add new products and stores. Its functional structure is hierarchical but not in a traditional sense. Layers of management are minimal, and staff members meet and work in small groups — small enough to meet the "two pizza rule," meaning two pizzas are enough to feed them. Despite its large size and hierarchical structure, Amazon is able to respond quickly to marketplace and strategic changes.

Figure 2.1 lists the major functions of Amazon's structure, showing how people and operations are grouped together into functions. Each function has a dedicated team answering to a senior manager. The hierarchical nature of the structure supports Amazon's aggressive growth strategy, allowing rapid expansion at managerial direction. The functional structure provides many advantages for Amazon and other single-line-of-business companies:

Knowledge sharing. Grouping employees together, especially those with specialized knowledge, promotes collaboration and skill development. As part of the same department, people have frequent contact with each other, and can easily share ideas and confer with one another. People in a functional unit are part of a well-defined community and have strong identity with their "professional" group.

Specialization. A functional structure allows for specialization in particular areas of expertise. Creating a department of lawyers allows them to specialize in different areas, such as contract law or labor law, and build a depth of knowledge that is available to the entire organization. If they are dispersed among the business units, then each will tend to be a generalist, needing to know a little about everything but without the opportunity to develop true expertise in any one area. The opportunity to specialize may also support professional career advancement as individuals gain expertise and marketable skills.

Leverage with vendors. A functional department that has common needs can present one face to the vendor. Its coordinated buying power can allow it to negotiate better contracts and prices.

Economies of scale. Particularly in manufacturing and production, where equipment can be extremely expensive, grouping people into functions can provide economies of scale. For example, if all testing is performed in one department, a single piece of equipment can be shared across product lines.

Office of the CEO

Business development

Amazon Web Services
(AWS)

Finance

International
consumer business

Accounting

Consumer business

Legal and secretariat

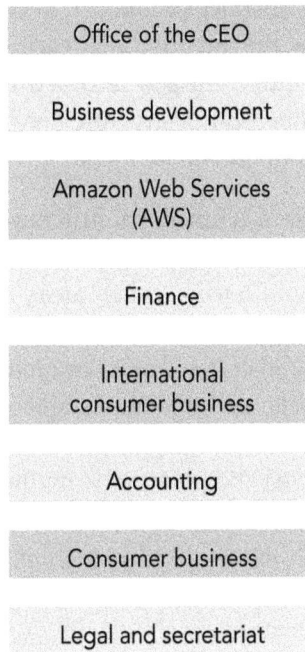

Figure 2.1 Functional groups on Amazon's organizational structure.

Standardization. A functional structure reduces duplication and divergence in systems and procedures. For example, a central information technology (IT) function sets documentation standards, which are then used for development projects throughout the organization. If IT is not grouped together as a function (or coordinated through strong lateral processes, teams, or policies), each business unit may set its own policies. When systems need to be shared or developed across business lines, the lack of common standards can become a source of conflict.

Amazon has expanded globally to more than 500,000 employees and continues to grow its operations, as well as its product offerings (e.g., Amazon Web Services, Whole Foods). As it increases the complexity of its business, it may encounter the two significant disadvantages of functional structures:

Managing diverse products or services. A functional structure is most effective for managing a single product or service line. Once the company branches into multiple, distinct product or service lines, a functional structure may not allow the attention that each requires. For example, Sony offers electronic equipment and recorded music services. To be a leader in each product line, Sony's structure needs to provide functional services and resources around both of these products lines.

Cross-functional processes. A functional structure tends to create barriers between different functional areas. The very strength of a specialized focus becomes a source of tension when areas must collaborate. Each area develops a unique, and often inward-focused, perspective. The classic example is the conflict between sales areas, which want to push ahead with new products, and operations areas, which are concerned about their ability to deliver on the promises made to customers. Although both areas have valid points of view, the result can be gridlock rather than collaboration. Decisions continually get pushed up to more senior executives for mediation, thereby creating bottlenecks and delays in decision-making and preventing mid-level managers from gaining decision-making experience.

If the organization has a single product or service that does not often change, it can afford the long cycle times that occur while functional units negotiate across these boundaries; however, this setting is unlikely in an innovative organization. When speed is required to enable cross-functional business processes, such as new product development, conflicts can render the functional structure ineffective. Since speed to market and product diversity are critical aspects of successful innovation, a straight functional structure provides few advantages for most organizations wishing to develop a structure that drives innovation.

The term *functional structure* is seen by some as a synonym for outmoded, traditional, or hierarchical organizations. It is frequently contrasted with images of fluid, flexible organizations populated by empowered employees. Although the functional structure does have limitations, it is no more hierarchical than any other structure. Hierarchy is a result of the number and nature of management levels, distribution of power, strength of integrative processes across organizational boundaries, and overall organizational culture. The functional structure should not be dismissed out of hand simply because it doesn't feel new. For some organizations, it can effectively drive innovation and be the preferred design option.

The Vertical Organization

The vertical organization, prevalent in the 1950s and 1960s, existed to manage specific functional competencies. It focused on functional performance, and used a small and centralized corporate staff to make decisions for the labor and production workforce, which made up 70% to 80% of the total workforce. Planning was organizationally separated from execution. Steps in the work process were distinct and aligned with specific jobs.

The vertical organization is based on a military style of monitoring and controlling performance, which originated centuries ago. Way back when Moses led the Jews out of Israel, he organized them in groups of 10. The leader of each group reported to another group of 10, and so on (Exodus 18:19-21). It rests on a very rigid and narrow definition of an individual's duties and a strict translation of the proper span of control. In the traditional military model, each soldier is assigned a specific task. One soldier is responsible for loading the gun on the right side of the ship; another is responsible for aiming it. A third is responsible for firing the gun.

This process works smoothly, even though each soldier performs only a small part of the overall process. The tasks are sequential and discrete, and there are clear and specific procedures and communications protocols to coordinate individuals and groups. As long as the process or technology remained stable and constant, this model worked extremely well.

In addition, commanding officers serve not only as vehicles for maintaining control and performance, but they also are responsible for transferring knowledge. Commanding officers have worked their way up through the ranks and usually have technical and functional expertise, which they transfer to their subordinates. Like the military model, hierarchy is the foundation of knowledge transfer in the vertical organization.

Since the required tasks in an industrial organization were seen as analogous to the division of labor in the military, the military structure seemed to be a perfect model for organizations to follow. In fact, industrial operations performed well for many years with this structure. However, as environments became more dynamic and knowledge transfer across the organization more important, new structures were needed to manage the more complex operations. The need for greater skill sets and cross-functional expertise increased, and organizations have begun to adopt more decentralized, network-based structures in recent years.

The Bureaucratic Organization

Over time, corporate organizations grew to accommodate their successes. For instance, automobile manufacturers increased production volume and added models and features. Additional machines were required to produce the increased volume and diversity of products. More machines required more people to run them, which, in turn, required more people to manage the people who were running them.

Next came the policies and procedures required to coordinate and control the additional size of the workforce and the complexity of the tasks. And in a never-ending upward spiral, more people were needed to develop and manage the new policies and procedures. As such, success drove vertical corporate organizations into bureaucratic organizations.

For the vertical organization, jobs were created to take responsibility for specific aspects of the work process. In the bureaucratic organization, jobs and additional layers of management were created to take responsibility for coordination of specific business processes and policies. Individual judgment, accountability, and empowerment were reduced.

Bureaucratic organizations, characterized by multiple layers of management and broad-reaching policies and procedures, were usually unable to respond effectively to rapid changes in the marketplace. Many corporations came to realize that as the size and complexity of the organization increased, so did the costs of maintaining a centralized bureaucracy to support the organization. The organization became inwardly focused on its own bureaucracy rather than outward on its customers and external environment. As the need to be more responsive to the market became evident, organizations took to restructuring again.

THE DECENTRALIZED ORGANIZATION

To address the challenges of the vertically structured, highly bureaucratic organization, the next logical move was simply to break big organizations into smaller ones. As a result, organizations began to divide themselves into decentralized units, with each unit a profit center reporting directly to an operations manager. Generally, each unit had complete authority, within "corporate guidelines," to create whatever policies and procedures were needed to maintain profitability and generate adequate returns to shareholders. In the pharmaceutical industry, for example, many companies divided their organization into units, each responsible for a different class of drugs or category of disease.

Decentralization provides several advantages. Smaller business units tend to be more flexible and are therefore more responsive to market demands. Additionally, smaller business units usually require less managerial overhead. However, the coordination is less effective between these independent units as compared to divisions within a more centralized organization. Responsiveness is gained at the costs of coordination.

As such, decentralized organizations often face a problem presenting a unified message to customers. A common scenario is multiple salespeople attempting to service the same account, with none of them able to provide a full line of solutions in a seamless manner. Two divisions of a leading automotive parts supplier were not only competing with each other for the same customers, but they were unknowingly being played off against each other to lower their prices. Please note, however, that the move to a decentralized business unit structure creates little change in the basic operational structure of most organizations. It simply breaks big organizations into small ones. The guiding principles of organizational structure—span of control, task specialization, functional silos, and knowledge transfer through the supervisor—do not normally change.

The decision to centralize or decentralize involves several considerations:

Abilities of lower-level managers. Decentralization assumes that capable managers with relevant experience are available at subordinate organizational levels. If a shortage exists, the tendency is to centralize. This, however, presents a dilemma because managers in a centralized environment may never reach their potential unless they are able to make important decisions more typical of a decentralized one. Moreover, managers who want to get more involved in the decision-making process may leave.

Cost and risk. The tendency to centralize is strong when decisions significantly affect the organization, and their costs and risks are high.

Environmental stability. As the organizational environment becomes more dynamic, decentralizing becomes more prevalent in meeting the needs of the organization.

External environment factors. Impact from external factors, e.g., governmental legislation; unions; federal, state, and local tax policies; and variations in economic trends and culture in the countries where the organization operates, often drive decentralization to respond to competition. As the external environment becomes more complex and dispersed, organizations are more likely to decentralize.

Growth of the organization. For organizations that are experiencing significant growth, making all decisions in one location or in one head is nearly impossible. This may require building decentralization into the organization's strategies and plans, and delegating decision-making to lower levels as situations, problems, and opportunities develop.

Management philosophies. Some managers and organizations pride themselves on making all the important decisions, while others pride themselves on delegating such decisions to subordinate managers. One can attribute the choice to a manager's past decision-making successes based on precedent, need, or personal preference.

Type or nature of the work. Depending on the type or nature of the work, along with the aforementioned considerations, multiple organizational forms may better suit the work. For example, some centralized support functions could conceivably support decentralized line functions more effectively.

Decentralization served organizations well until global competition and customer satisfaction became critical drivers of success. It was time to consider alternative structures.

Geographic Structure

A geographic structure is organized around physical locations such as states, countries, or regions. A geographic structure operates best in a complex but stable environment or in a simple but dynamic environment. The geographic structure is best for companies that:

- Have a high cost of transport

- Deliver service on-site

- Need to be physically close to customers for delivery or support

- Need to create a perception that the organization is "local"

The suitability of a geographic structure is highly dependent on whether you need to be close to the source of your products or to your customers. Cement companies have high transportation costs for their products and tend to organize geographically near quarries. Chains of hair stylists and restaurants require their customers to physically come to them, so they need to be located close to those customers.

A national pizza chain provides a good example of a geographic structure. The company is grouped into northern, central, and southern regions. Each region is large enough to support its own functional organization at the next level. These regional organizations operate independently and are able to serve local needs and customs. However, two functions—purchasing and real estate—are centralized and shared by all regions. The reason for this is that the staples of the pizza business—flour, cheese, and tomato sauce—can be purchased more efficiently when prices are negotiated with national vendors. Maintaining consistency while ensuring freshness makes a streamlined, efficient distribution supply chain a core organizational capability for the company. In addition, site selection, leasing, and management of real estate require specialized expertise. It makes more sense for these specialists to work together than to have their knowledge diluted across the regions.

The geographic structure provides one clear advantage:

Local focus. A geographic structure is important when culture, language, or political factors influence buying patterns and differ significantly by region. For example, within Amazon's functional organization described earlier, geographic divisions, including North America and international, are maintained to address the specific customs, laws, and marketplace needs for the region (Meyer 2019a).

The geographic structure often poses one distinct disadvantage:

Mobilizing and sharing resources. The geographic structure gives power to the regional or country manager. As soon as a customer needs a "global" solution requiring talent from multiple regions, the geographic structure slows down response time. Consider a large enterprise-technology consulting firm organized by country. A Spanish bank announces it will be outsourcing the management of its IT around the world. It puts out a request for bids. The managing partner of the consulting firm located in Spain begins what he calls the "begging process" of asking other country managers to free up people and send them to Madrid to work on the proposal. During the two weeks it takes to mobilize this team, a competitor, with profit centers organized around customer segments such as banking, has already completed its bid. When a company is organized by country or regional profit centers, the power to allocate a limited resource (in this case, talent) resides with the geographic manager.

Advances in technology reduce the importance of location for geographically based organizations. Many historically local companies, e.g., bookstores, movie rentals, have been forced to close or make significant changes to their business models in the face of more distant vendors that can ship products direct to your door. In healthcare, use of remote-care technology has allowed care providers to communicate with patients and provide treatment regimens without either having to travel. The need for expensive local facilities is reduced, patients benefit from more timely services, and physicians can use their time more efficiently.

Being "local" may no longer provide an advantage. On other fronts, Internet-based learning programs have expanded the reach of colleges to new customers. Online banking allows banks to decrease the cost of building and maintaining branches. If the company's product can be easily and quickly transported or delivered, geography does not necessarily provide an advantage. Semiconductor plants need to be located where there is skilled labor, not necessarily close to raw material suppliers or clients. Credit-card call centers can be located anywhere as long as the employee shifts cover a range of time zones.

Product Structure

The product structure is organized into product divisions. Each division has its own functional structure to support its products. A product structure operates best in a complex but stable environment or in a simple but dynamic environment. The product structure is best for companies that:

- Compete based on product features or being first in the market

- Produce multiple products for separate market segments

- Produce products with short life cycles; speed in product development time is an advantage

- Have a large enough organization to achieve the minimum efficient scale required to duplicate across the organization

A product structure often evolves from a functional structure when a company diversifies its product or service lines and each line is large enough to support its own production. As the company grows, it continually subdivides divisions. As each division becomes large enough to support multiple product lines, it is subdivided further. For example, a medical equipment company may have three divisions: electronic instruments, medical instruments, and handheld computers. The medical instruments division is divided into imaging, measurement devices, and therapeutic devices. Each of these is further subdivided by product. Each product line has its own R&D, operations, and marketing functions. The company's electronic instruments and handheld computers divisions are spin-offs from the main division of medical instruments that allow the company to leverage its experience with small computing and electronic devices to create equipment aimed at the medical market.

Structuring by product line allows a clear focus on developing new product features and variations. Since each product line has access to its own support, it can focus on R&D and compress its new product cycle time without regard to what else is occurring in the organization. The product structure has three primary advantages over the functional structure.

Product development cycle. By having each division on a single product or service line, the ability to design or redesign products end-to-end is compressed, which is an important benefit in markets where buyers expect new products or significant enhancements to be continually introduced. The PC industry is a good example of a product that competes based on rapid product development cycles.

Product excellence. Structuring by product line also allows an organization to focus on innovation and product improvement. Each R&D division is narrowly focused on its line of products.

Broad operating freedom. The divisions in product companies usually have a high degree of autonomy. The head of each division is a general manager with complete responsibility for everything that goes on in that division. This freedom allows each division to pursue opportunities or new directions without the constraint of coordinating with other divisions.

The product structure introduces some challenges as well:

Divergence. In a product structure, division managers are essentially running their own business and may even see themselves as being in competition with other division managers. In the example given, the imaging equipment product line developed a new scanning technology. At the same time, the handheld computer division was looking for scanning features to incorporate into its computer products. However, since the research departments work independently, the managers in handheld computers did not find out about the scanning technology until it was released into the market. They lost valuable months of R&D time. The narrow focus of R&D within the product unit may also lead to complacency and a lack of new insights needed for innovation.

Duplication. Each functional area is duplicated across the company and is more strongly aligned to the division it supports than the broader functional community. Standards, policies, and procedures diverge, and efforts may be duplicated. Strong lateral processes avoid this duplication of resource expenditure.

Lost economies of scale. By dividing functions across product or service lines, economies of scale are lost. One solution is to create a hybrid structure where multiple product lines share a centralized function. Sometimes also called a "shared service," the shared function allows for greater depth of expertise and efficiency. This was illustrated in the example of the shared purchasing function for the national pizza chain discussed previously.

Multiple customer points of contact. The product structure can create multiple points of contact for customers who buy more than one product from the company. Banking companies typically offer multiple products that may be accessed in multiple ways by their customers. Each access point and each product will follow a different customer journey. The front-end systems must allow the customer to access all products through one portal—their access point of choice. This customer expectation must be considered in the organizational structure and may pose a challenge in a product-driven structure (Price 2019; Maechler et al. 2018).

Customer Structure

The customer structure is organized around major market segments such as client groups, industries, or population groups. The customer structure is best for companies that:

- Compete in market segments in which buyers have strength and influence over the market

- Can use customer knowledge to provide an advantage

- Compete based on rapid customer service and product cycle times

- Have a large enough organization to achieve the minimum efficient scale required to duplicate functions

While functional and product organizations have internal advantages, they don't necessarily provide an easy interface to the customer. What is a simple and rational structure for managers may be cumbersome and complex for clients. For example, AT&T is divided organizationally into separate businesses around its products of wireless cell phone services, local service, long distance, and Internet access. A customer might believe that buying all these services through AT&T would confer some benefits — perhaps simplified billing or discounts. In fact, a complex structure such as this makes it difficult for a customer service representative or salesperson working in one AT&T business to be able to provide information about other products across the company, much less access billing records or resolve problems. As a result, customer satisfaction suffers, and smaller, less complex companies, such as Ting, begin to take on the larger companies (Fowler 2019).

Organizational structures based on customer, market, or industry segments make it easy for the buyer to do business with the organization. For service businesses that must intimately know the preferences of their clients to stay competitive, organizing by market segment makes sense. While Marriott International is a large, multifaceted company, it is also a good example of an organization that has chosen to primarily organize itself around distinct market segments, such as lodging, ownership resorts, and senior living. For example, within its lodging business, Marriott has further segmented the market into full-service hotels and extended-stay facilities. Marriott collects extensive information regarding its customers' preferences, so that on return stays, a visit can be customized down to the types of pillows on the beds.

The customer structure meets a number of growing needs for organizations, particularly those in service businesses:

Customization. Buyers increasingly expect customized products and services in exchange for their business. They are realizing the power they have to influence their suppliers, and the trends toward preferred providers, outsourcing, and contracting are declining. In addition, technology is allowing for more "mass customization" in both products and services. For example, most news organizations provide online news updates and summaries based on settings that are defined by the user —

the user decides when and how often, as well as the kind of content he or she wishes to receive. Music customers can set up customized playlists based on music sites such as Spotify, selecting the genre of music they want to listen to by specific times of the day; the music they want for their exercise regimen may be different from the music they want for their evening meal. The era of big data and artificial intelligence has greatly expanded capabilities for mass customization.

Relationships. If long relationships and repeat business are important, customer structures provide an advantage. For example, a bank's customer-service call center takes calls from a variety of bank customers. Although the call center ultimately supports the buyers of the bank's products, the call center exists to meet the needs of its internal customers — the managers who run the bank's divisions. Therefore, the call center's managers customize their services for their internal customers (e.g., scripts, wait time, follow-up service). Knowledge of the customer and responsiveness can keep an internal activity from being outsourced. It can also keep an external supplier as a preferred vendor.

Solutions. More and more organizations are finding that their customers want solutions, not just individual products. They want products bundled with services, such as consulting, advice, training, or follow-up technical support. Gathering these capabilities in the organization and presenting them to customers in an integrated, attractively priced package is a challenge if they are located in a variety of divisions. The customer organization puts information and power in the hands of those employees who interact with and understand the unique needs of each customer or market segment (see also Chapter 7).

The customer structure poses the same challenges as the product structure:

Divergence. Knowledge and standards do not get shared across customer segments.

Duplication. Development efforts may be duplicated.

Scale. Opportunities for leveraging scale are lost.

These challenges can be addressed through strong lateral connections and by centralizing some common functions or services. A computer manufacturer that uses the same part across product and customer lines will benefit from a shared purchasing function that can pool purchases or negotiate the best prices with suppliers.

COMBINING MODELS

Often, an organization adopts a mash-up of structures; this may be due to legacy decisions accumulating over time, but it can be a useful approach when redesigning structure. It is unlikely that one structure type will be the "end all be all" for any given company. Understanding the unique needs of an organization and then pulling from successful elements of more than one model is a reasonable approach to finding the most effective structure. Starbucks Coffee Company, with its coffee shops located around the world, uses a functional structure that includes both geographic and product components (Meyer 2019c; Meyer 2019d; Mohr 2019). Functions such as HR, finance, and marketing are part of the hierarchical functional structure, while its coffee shops are organized by geographical region (e.g., Americas, China/Asia Pacific, and Europe/Middle Asia/Africa), and its products are organized by lines (e.g., coffee, baked goods, merchandise). This structure operates in a matrix fashion and supports the company's ability to be innovative through the intersections of these structures. The structure allows Starbucks to provide a continued focus on customer experience while expanding the business through acquisitions and new stores.

Front-Back Hybrid Structure

The front-back hybrid structure combines elements of both the product and customer structures to provide the benefits of both. It allows for product excellence at the back end while increasing customer satisfaction at the front end. The front-back hybrid structure is best for organizations that:

- Are large and have multiple product lines and market segments
- Serve global customers and must have cross-border coordination
- Need to maximize both customer and product excellence
- Have managers skilled in managing complexity

The front-back structure bears special discussion because it addresses many of the disadvantages posed by other structures. It also introduces complexity into the design. Both the front-end customer organization and the back-end product organizations are multifunction profit centers. This is what distinguishes them from the other types of structures in which the profit centers are either geographically oriented or enterprise-wide (e.g., functional).

A global commercial bank is a good example, where the front-back structure allows the company to focus on global customers across borders. The front-end is segmented by industry and then by client. Local account managers are assigned to countries where the client has a major presence. Local account managers build local relationships and deal with local delivery issues. The global account managers coordinate the overall delivery of service to the client.

Each industry group has its own profit and loss (P&L) accountability and includes functions such as sales, service, and local marketing. Each group sells the company's products in ways tailored to its unique purchasing needs. They also use the knowledge gained by having an industry focus to feed new product ideas back to the product organization.

The front-end organizations draw upon the resources of the back-end organizations. As "buyers" of the product, they can ask for customization to meet the unique needs of their customers.

The back end is segmented by product line—cash management, foreign exchange, and corporate finance—each with P&L responsibility as well. In this example, each product is large enough to have dedicated functional support (operations, IT, marketing, etc.) If the organization did not have such scale, these functions could be shared across product lines.

The front-back structure meets several of the needs organizations have today:

Single point of interface for customers. This is when customers are buyers of multiple products but want a single point of interface and one account. Although complex on the inside, the front-back structure creates a simple and clear interface with customers. They have one account for all their products, and no matter what distribution channel they choose, all information is available.

Cross-selling. New customer acquisition is expensive. It is more profitable to sell more and different products to existing customers and develop long-term relationships with them than to find new ones. A front-back organization allows the sales channels to cross-sell and bundle products because databases and technology allow them to access complete information about existing customers.

Value-added systems and solutions. A customer who plans to build a trading room needs someone who will sell him or her more than excellent computers. The customer is in the market for consulting advice, implementation support, and service contracts, as well as equipment. These are all front-end services that can add considerable value to commoditized products.

Product focus. The front-back structure preserves the product divisions that allow for innovation, product excellence, and sustained product development that characterize a product structured company. In the bank example, the cash management, foreign exchange, and corporate finance divisions have the support and focus that allow them to compete with top rivals in the industry.

Multiple distribution channels. Almost every company today is developing an Internet strategy to allow it to sell products directly over the internet. Companies that are already organized around customers find it easier to move to e-commerce than those that are organized by product. Rather than completely shifting focus, the front-back model allows the product-focused company to present a new, integrated face to the customer.

The front-back structure also introduces complexity into the design that, if not managed, can overwhelm the organization:

Contention over resources. If the front-end unit is a small geographic or market segment, it may not be able to get attention from the back-unit (e.g., adjustment in production schedules, customization of product features, pursuit of a new customer opportunity). Conversely, back-end units may be frustrated when trying to get front-end units to promote products or address functional priorities (e.g., resources for launching new systems or cost-saving changes).

Disagreements over prices and customer needs. Front-end units are likely to push for price concessions to win new business, or they may ask for highly expensive customization to meet a preferred customer's need. The back-end units will be focused on maintaining prices and margins. They may try to push products out to customers whether they are appropriate or not to maintain product profitability.

These conflicts will require clear processes for resolution, as well as managers who are skilled enough to negotiate solutions that are for the good of the company rather than for just their own unit.

Determining the placement of marketing. In a front-back hybrid structure, it may be difficult to determine where marketing belongs, and it is often split into two parts. In the bank example, product marketing (e.g., cash management) would be placed in the back end. Segment marketing (e.g., automotive) would go in the front end. Coordinating the efforts of these marketing groups and avoiding having anything "sit in the middle" becomes another challenge.

Conflicting metrics. Front-end units will measure success in terms of speed, agility, and ability to customize solutions, while the back-end units will focus on scale, uniformity, integration, and efficiency. These conflicts will drive different behaviors within each part of the company, which will need to be recognized and managed.

Information and accounting complexity. This structure is heavily dependent on shared information and accounting systems to ensure both ends have the same access to data. The multiple and sometimes overlapping P&Ls require transaction and accounting systems that credit income, allocate expenses, and generate management information system (MIS) reports from multiple perspectives.

One company that has experimented with a front-back structure is Hewlett-Packard (HP). Throughout much of its 80-plus year history, HP had been organized in a product structure with multiple, independently run product units. Products were developed with little internal collaboration on how they could be packaged together to create more value and new markets. In recent years, the structure has been updated to combine the product units into two back-end organizations: computers, and printing and imaging equipment. The front-end unit, restructured in 2019 into a single commercial organization that comprises 10 geographic regions (Alspach 2019), is responsible for sales and contractual agreements. This restructuring is intended to "simplify operating models, enable more digitally supported transactions, and deliver better value proposition to HP's customers."

The Matrix Organization

In the matrix structure, the functional portions of the organizational structure are loosely linked together along customer or product lines. More commonly found in project-based organizations, the matrix organizational structure has had mixed results. Although the matrix organization allows for enhanced customer focus while maintaining functional integrity, the structure typically has been associated with increased organization tension and confusion surrounding dual reporting relationships.

Although a matrix organization exists in several variations, the easiest description is that of a product structure superimposed on a functional structure. In this design, an employee has more than one supervisor: the functional supervisor and the project manager (PM). For it to work effectively, key managers must agree on a balance or sharing of power over resources. Conflict resolution must also occur openly and frequently to resolve inevitable disagreements. If organizationally advantageous, the PM should also have the authority when conflicts arise to set priorities for the individual's work schedule. This structure operates best in a complex and dynamic environment.

Whether viewed as a success or as a failure, the matrix organizational structure has been hampered by the management thinking and technologies of the past. However, recent changes in each of these have allowed the network organization to emerge as a successful structural alternative to the matrix approach.

THE NETWORK ORGANIZATION

The most recent stage in organizational structure development, the network organization, represents the real innovation in the design of organizational structure, and it is quickly becoming the preferred structure for high-performing, innovative companies. The network organization has its roots in the matrix structures of the past. In the network organizational structure, the focus is on the customer and not on internal business functions. By focusing externally, rather than internally, networked organizations are better positioned to be more responsive to the total needs of their customers and changes in the market.

Network organizations are based on teams of people handling a process or serving a client, rather than on individuals performing functional tasks under several layers of management. The emergence of network organizations is a direct consequence of two major changes in management thinking. The first change is an understanding of the importance of a multiskilled workforce. This change in management thinking rejects Adam Smith's notion that ultimate benefits come from the division of labor. The second change is a realization that business success is not based purely on technical or functional expertise, but rather on applying these to the processes and resources that are required to meet customer needs. (See Chapter 6 for more information on network structures.)

How does the organizational chart need to change? The transformation from traditional structures is primarily a shift from hierarchical structures to ever-shifting networks. The organizational chart loses its permanence and gets rewritten regularly and frequently—as often as teams form, conduct their work, and then reform to go on to other work. Gone are the days of specific job descriptions and defined, non-overlapping job responsibilities. The role of "other duties as assigned" is becoming the primary job responsibility, rather than the catch-all phrase often found at the bottom of the job description, and it's becoming "other duties as the need arises."

Structuring the organization to focus on networks can be revolutionary and is not without challenges. A network-focused structure means less hierarchy, fewer job descriptions, and a different approach to management. Disruptive changes to the organizational structure are often required to get to disruptive innovations. However, the network models proven to enhance the innovation structure are characterized by leveraging networks that already exist informally throughout the organization. See Appendix B, Organizational Network Analysis, for more information.

The factors contributing to the need for flexible and efficient organizations are not new. Why then, has it taken so long to develop this structural response? Major trends that have set the scene for the evolution of the network structure are advances in IT and the transition to a service economy.

Information Technology

Information technology is one of the most important enablers of network organizations because it:

1. Breaks the organization's dependence on "expert" managers

2. Permits people to work together as a team regardless of geographic boundaries

3. Empowers people to participate in and coordinate the work process at different points in time and in different ways

Traditionally, expertise has belonged to the employee, and knowledge transfer has been provided on a need-to-know basis by functional or technical experts. Employees became more valuable based on what knowledge or experience they had. With the advent of expert systems and knowledge-based software packages, expertise is no longer monopolized by a few people. It is stored in computer databases and available to anyone with minimal computer knowledge and access to a PC. Expertise is shifted from being a personal asset to a corporate asset.

For example, HR departments have typically required specialists in making compensation and benefits decisions. Now, a HR generalist can take advantage of an expert system or a decision support tool to find and hire the right talent or to deal with a compensation or benefit issue. Similarly, workers on the factory floor who used to rely on their supervisor for workflow or inventory information now have that information available to them when they need it through electronic interfaces located at their workstations.

Technology has allowed organizations to take spans of control to new extremes and dimensions. Managers can now oversee employees and business operations located in different parts of the world. Aided by advances in portable communications and computing technology, a sales manager can communicate and interface with sales personnel scattered across a broad geographic region.

Global communications, groupware, and other technological innovations allow individuals and groups of individuals to not only work in a coordinated fashion from different points on the globe but also at different points in time. Work that previously required sequential processes can now be conducted in parallel through enhanced communications and coordination. Messages can be posted to an electronic system and be received and replied to at different points in time. A team of people can work on a project continuously from sites on opposite sides of the globe.

Through the sharing of expertise and information, managers no longer need to be involved with task control and resolution of short-term issues. Managers can then devote more time to planning, organizing, and supporting their teams with information and guidance. The result is an organization that is flatter and more flexible.

As a result of the changes in technology, employees can make better business decisions and stay informed on the progress of the whole process. No longer are they limited to their "little corner of the world." Consequently, their jobs can be broader. Technology also allows mechanisms to capture ideas and pain points from many sources, including front-line employees, feeding the innovation process (see Chapter 5, Technology, and Appendix B, Opportunity Centers). With technology, employees can truly work smarter.

Service Economy

The traditional models of organizational structure utilized in the industrial segment were soon discovered to be less than effective in the emerging service sector. This was partially because tasks in service organizations are not normally as distinct or as repetitive as those in the industrial sector. This fluctuation in tasks is often a direct consequence of the interaction service employees have with their customers.

For example, bank tellers handle a variety of transactions, each of which can be complicated by the customer. One customer may not have a deposit slip. Another wants to split the deposit between two accounts. A third wants to transfer money from one account into another. Each transaction is technically a deposit; however, the actual tasks vary and require careful attention to the individual needs of each customer.

Services may be transactional, as in the bank example; ongoing, i.e., delivered repeatedly on a regular basis, such as routine dental care; or continual and without interruption, e.g., power supply. The shift from a manufacturing economy to a service economy has emphasized the need for skilled employees who can rapidly and efficiently deal with an array of customer needs across these sectors. Customers are no longer satisfied to move from point to point to receive services in business models that place the burdens of organizational bureaucracy and cumbersome procedures on them.

Customers now expect that businesses meet their unique wants and needs on demand and on the spot. The ability to provide these levels of services becomes a competitive differentiator. Rather than moving from station to station within a bank, customers expect the teller to be able to handle all their needs right then and there. The role of the service worker is now to serve as the interface between customers with random needs and the organization's processes, policies, and procedures. In the context of the service economy, the narrowly defined jobs and roles of the past no longer make sense.

This shift to a service economy has also increased the need for organizations to better understand and satisfy the needs of their customers. Direct competition for customers has increased the importance of maintaining a strong sense of customer focus. The one-size-fits-all model of business no longer makes competitive sense. The bureaucracies, processes, and structures that were designed for efficient, mass production are no longer enough to effectively satisfy customers on an individual basis. See Chapter 7, Structuring for Service Innovation.

Two popular models of network structure are currently being implemented in organizations: case management and horizontal process management.

Case Management Network Structure

Case management is an increasingly popular organizational structure design that can overcome many of the disadvantages of more traditional structures. Case management was pioneered in the healthcare industry in response to the importance of patient service and relatively high levels of service and organizational complexity. In many healthcare organizations, clinical care teams are assigned to track a patient through his or her stay in the hospital to manage the entire process, or case, of patient care delivery.

Case management does not eliminate functional divisions within an organization; rather, it facilitates the coordination of the functions in which one person takes the responsibility and ownership of an individual case from beginning to end. Four key components of successful case management are (Davenport and Nohria 1994):

1. A "closed-loop" work process that involves completion or management of an entire customer product or service

2. A location in the organizational structure at the intersection of the customer and the various other functions or units that create or deliver the customer product or service

3. Empowerment and role expansion of employees to make decisions and address customer issues

4. Easy electronic access to information located throughout the organization and the use of IT to aid in decision-making

Horizontal Process Management Network Structure

A step beyond case management toward cross-functional integration is horizontal process management with its own set of advantages. In this situation, an organization examines its core processes and designs a structure that encompasses all the requirements necessary to meet the customer needs of that service process. Some typical core processes are:

- New product design

- Order fulfillment

- Order entry

- New product introduction

- After-sale service

- Supplier partnerships

In some ways, it is similar to a matrix organization; however, the solid-line relationship is to the process and the dotted-line relationship is to the function rather than vice versa.

The goal is not to make a complete horizontal process organization. Rather, each organization should seek its own unique balance between the vertical and horizontal features that are needed to deliver performance.

At the heart of horizontal process organizations are these 10 principles:

1. Organize around processes not tasks

2. Flatten hierarchy by minimizing the subdivision of workflows and non-value-added activities

3. Assign ownership of process and process performance

4. Link performance objectives and evaluation to customer satisfaction

5. Make teams, not individuals, the principal building blocks of organization performance design

6. Combine managerial and non-managerial activities as often as possible

7. Treat multiple competencies as the rule not the exception

8. Inform and train people on a just-in-time-to-perform basis rather than a need-to-know basis

9. Maximize supplier and customer contact

10. Reward individual skill development and team performance, not just individual performance

IMPLEMENTATION OF NETWORK STRUCTURE

Implementing a network structure has many ramifications for organizations. Reorganizing to a network structure affects many other aspects of the organizations as well, including:

1. Management style

2. Performance management systems

3. Education and training programs

4. Communications processes

5. Compensation and rewards programs

6. Management development

Once you decide to adopt a network organization, the structural change is just the tip of the iceberg.

Management Style

Implementing any model of network structure in an organization requires a fundamental shift in management style for most people. For some, this shift often results in managers having to learn a different way of doing business in their organization. For others, particularly those who are adept at managing projects with cross-functional teams, their management style will require little or no modification. But, for most, the answer rests in the middle.

This shift is not an elimination of a manager's responsibilities. Managers still need to have a high level of involvement but with a different focus. Rather than peering over the shoulder of each individual, managers need to monitor the progress of the team, with an eye toward improving the team's decision-making ability. As Tom Davenport, partner at Ernst & Young, notes, "The case manager should not operate without any controls, but excessive control over case management defeats the key purpose of the initiative" (Davenport and Nohria 1994).

As a result, managers become leaders of teams by providing information and guidance to help them make decisions within the process. Process managers lead by supporting the team.

Performance Management

A network organization also requires changes in the performance management system. In functional organizations, employees are rewarded for moving up or deeper into a particular specialty. In network organizations, this need not be the case. Rather, the ultimate measure of success is "How satisfied is the customer?" Rather than being assessed only on individual competence, the measure may include how well individual competence was applied toward the total satisfaction of the customer, as well as the team's contribution to their organization's strategic goals.

Education and Training

Organizations must provide additional training to support the network structure. If employees are required to perform broader tasks and are responsible for making on-the-spot decisions, additional training may be necessary not only for each new skill required, but also for improvement of communication skills and teamwork. This poses many potential problems for organizations, particularly when selecting or training entry-level employees. Who will be trained? What will they be trained in? How much is the optimal level of training? Do you buy or train the talent you need?

Communication System

For the teams within a network structure to properly function, an open communications environment must exist. Process information, business data, and organizational strategy are just a few of the subjects that need to be at everyone's fingertips. When teams in a network organization are expected to make good business decisions, the quality of their decision-making will be directly proportional to the quality of information they have. See Chapters 5 and 8 for information on the knowledge management system (KMS). They need direct communications links with customers and suppliers as well.

Compensation and Benefits

Multiskilled individuals with team and customer focuses need to be recognized, reinforced, and rewarded in network organizations. As such, the new organizational rewards system must be able to accommodate this shift. Various pay for performance, pay for skill, and productivity bonus systems in the modern organization have grown out of this need.

Additionally, in a network organization, whether using a case management or process management approach, employees and the team need to be rewarded based on customer satisfaction, individual contribution to group performance, and overall organizational performance.

Management Development

With flatter organizations becoming a reality, the chances for advancement "up the corporate ladder" are drastically reduced. So how does an organization provide career opportunities for its employees? It does this by: (1) making lateral movement in an organization a desirable endeavor that is seen as a career success; and (2) realigning the goal setting, performance review, and career development processes to promote managers based on their ability to form and mobilize networks that serve customers rather than on building their own functional skills. Table 2.1 provides a summary overview of the advantages and disadvantages of the different organizational structures.

THE IMPORTANCE OF STRUCTURE

> *"We trained very hard, but it seems like every*
> *time we were beginning to form up into teams,*
> *we would be reorganized. I was to learn later on*
> *in life that we tend to meet any new situation by*
> *reorganizing. A wonderful method it can be for*
> *creating the illusion of progress while producing*
> *confusion, inefficiency, and demoralization."*
>
> – Charles Ogburn, Jr. (Ogburn 1957)

The organizational structure determines where formal power and authorities are located and is a key driver of organizational performance. It comprises the organization's components, its relationships, and its hierarchies, and it channels the energy of the organization and provides a home and identity for employees. The structure is what is shown in a typical organizational chart.

Is one structure better than another? Yes! Each of the structural types described, alone or in combination, is the best answer for a certain situation. While none of them are right for all occasions, one (or a combination) is right to improve organizational performance while focusing on developing an innovative culture.

Taking the time to identify the structure that is most likely to lead to an organization's desired performance is well worth the effort and can provide huge benefits. Reorganizing without a well-designed structure is more likely to lead to confusion, frustration, and wasted resources. However, it is important to note that there may be some trial and error involved, and no structure will last forever; implement the structure that is believed to be the best, but be ready to adjust or redirect when it becomes necessary.

Today's organizations must maximize innovation in each of five areas to truly succeed and prosper (MindTools Content Team, McKinsey 7-S Framework; McKinsey Quarterly, 2008):

1. Management

2. Process

3. Product

4. Sales and marketing

5. Services

A look at organizational structures that foster innovation in each of these areas follows in the succeeding chapters.

CHAPTER THREE

Structuring for Management Innovation

MANAGEMENT STRUCTURE'S RELATION TO INNOVATION

HOW WELL AN ORGANIZATION INNOVATES depends to a large degree on its culture, which in turn depends largely on its leadership and management styles. Organizational structure defines the division of activities and responsibilities, sets up communication lines (and barriers), and forms the basis of decision-making rules. Management is responsible for the organizational structure, and structure is a major contributor to the day-to-day operations that will either breathe life into innovative practices or doom them to the dustbin.

Well-known aspects of organizational structure include organizational divisions/departments; management/employee hierarchies, alignments, and areas of coordination; and communication and decision lines. The organizational chart is often used to illustrate the structure (see Appendix B, Organizational Chart). These structural aspects must be designed to drive innovation, and there are some key practices to accomplish this.

First and foremost, management must be structured to remain close to the customer and the customer experience. Isolation of management from the customer, whether due to too many layers between them, divisional barriers, or handing off those responsibilities to non-management, leads to a loss in focus on value creation and delighting those customers. Countless organizations have learned the hard way that customers will go elsewhere if their product or service needs are not met, and management disconnect may be the reason. Executives polled in a recent study by *The Economist* said that organizational, not technical, obstacles are the most likely to get in the way of better customer service (Kapoor and Koehring 2014). Of the 491 executives surveyed, 36% cited organizational siloes as their biggest challenge, and another 24% cited a lack of senior management vision. Clearly, management structure is a critical success factor for innovating and creating customer value.

How can management be structured to keep the customer experience front and center? Consider hiring a chief customer officer with senior-level responsibilities for coordinating the customer perspective across the organization. Add a single, integrated customer response unit with access to all units within the organization and responsibility for unifying the organization behind the customer experience. Assign responsibility for measuring the customer experience in a way that looks beyond simple sales histories and satisfaction surveys. Understanding customers' loyalties to the organization and its brand, as well as their influence on other customers and potential customers, will contribute significantly to creating value for those customers.

While keeping managers close to the customer experience is extremely important, the organization's management structure must also build an internal environment in which innovation thrives. Management structure must allow and encourage rapid pivots in direction when the business environment changes, without losing focus or drive. Using a structure that is flexible and capable of reprioritizing at a moment's notice is critical for identifying and capitalizing on new opportunities, as well as responding to unanticipated business disruptions.

Generally speaking, flatter is better when designing a management structure that allows the efficiency and agility needed for innovation. A key hallmark of Google's structure is its flatness (Smithson 2019). However, rigid adherence to any management structure is less likely to develop an organization in which employees are willing to take risks, another key success factor for innovation. Managers must be comfortable with failure and give their employees space to become comfortable with it, too.

> *"We don't want to just innovate by creating new products, we want to innovate by creating the culture that will allow for that innovation space to happen."*
>
> – David Skok, Digital Advisor (Silverman 2015)

As in any management structure, management must provide sufficient resources. In the world of innovation, this will likely require some changes from traditional resource allocation. For example, more open-ended resource commitments are necessary during the early phases of understanding customer needs and connecting them with innovative solutions. Getting to the deep understanding of customer needs and exploring new combinations of knowledge, technology, and models to arrive at an innovative solution is not something that can be fit into a prescribed bucket of time and money. Tight control of resources during this period risks losing out on finding the best, most value-creating solution and ending up with a failed attempt at innovation. As an innovative solution emerges and is developed and deployed, traditional project management will become more applicable.

Management structures best suited for innovation take a holistic approach, eliminating siloes in the organization. Business units are integrated as much as possible, and where handoffs are necessary, the processes for those handoffs ensure a collaborative and smooth transition. All the structure's components remain true to the organization's vision and strategic objectives. A fundamental culture of continuous improvement, quality, and risk management provides a firm basis on which to build a holistic innovation management structure.

> *"We are evolving our quality system to be a catalyst for innovation. Innovation must happen everywhere and in everything we do. From our products and services, to our systems and processes – our quality systems must encourage innovation at the speed of the Internet."*
>
> – Rodney Donaville, Senior Director, Customer Experience, Quality and Culture, HP

MANAGEMENT STRUCTURE MODELS FOR INNOVATION

Given that organizational structures play a significant role in effective innovation, what structural models have been shown to work? A look at several models used by organizations known to be successful innovators, some traditional and some more recently introduced, is informative.

Traditional Management Structures for Innovation

Organizations have long known they need to come up with new products and services and to continue to improve their processes and business models if they wish to remain competitive. Research and development departments have been popular for this purpose. In some organizations, the sales and marketing group is responsible for coming up with new products and services, and in others, a product management group does this. Occasionally, engineering or product development carries the bulk of the responsibility for identifying new product features. Should these functional structural models be avoided in today's world? Not necessarily. We'll look at the pros and cons of each of these models and then review some newer approaches.

Research and Development

In the R&D model, a dedicated unit in the organization, perhaps under its own management, is responsible for generating new ideas, vetting them, revising and enhancing them, and bringing them to production readiness. This model has been around for a long time and has worked well for many organizations. Sometimes referred to as "skunkworks," organizations such as Lockheed Martin, IBM, Google, DuPont, Ford, and Nike have used this approach (Hopkins 2016).

Benefits of the dedicated R&D unit are that it is independent from the day-to-day distractions of operations, allowing its personnel to focus its efforts and resources on the identification and development of cutting-edge solutions. Such a group may be very adept at keeping up with new technologies and how they can be incorporated into the organization's product and service portfolio. Downsides are that by being independent of other parts of the organization, the R&D group can become insular and disconnected from the core business. Without direct access to customers/users and their problems, the researchers may not be able to develop the deep relationships needed to identify customer needs and opportunities.

Sales and Marketing

Sales and marketing group(s) are responsible for bringing new ideas into the company in this model, targeting new products and markets, and forecasting the needs of the marketplace. Since this group is in closest touch with the customers and the marketplace, many organizations use these employees as their innovation generators. Knowing the issues customers face, what competitive forces are active in the marketplace, and where the most revenues may be gained can form the basis of the innovation pipeline.

Sales and marketing employees, however, will be incented first and foremost to make the sale. Generally, they tend to be "blue sky" without taking time for realistic risk/benefit assessments. Given that they must remain focused on the next sale, they may be limited in their ability to think more broadly about unmet needs, both current and future; issues the customers are facing; and new market opportunities.

Many companies create two separate departments for marketing and sales, each with very different responsibilities and accountabilities. Sales is responsible for meeting target sales volumes, while marketing is responsible for defining market regions and preparing market specifications to guide product development. Marketing is typically also responsible for creating the advertising campaign. In this organizational structure, it is absolutely imperative that sales and marketing maintain an effective way of exchanging information, new ideas, and customer pain points, even though they have different primary responsibilities.

Product Management

Product management groups take responsibility in some management structures for keeping a finger on the pulse of the marketplace, bringing together customers' needs and issues with new technology or other solutions, and then working with engineering to bring them to fruition. Product managers typically have connections with both the market/customer side and the engineering/product development side and can bridge the gaps between them. They become translators of the customers' concerns for the developers who can resolve them.

This model can suffer, however, when disruptive innovations compete with more minor (and less innovative) product tweaks and fixes. Resource constraints may lead the product manager to opt for the low-hanging fruit of the quick fix in order to offer a solution to customers in the short term, missing out on longer-term, higher-payoff innovations. The product manager may not have management authority over engineering and development and is therefore unable to champion innovations through development. Only a product manager who is highly skilled in relationship management can bring the balance needed in this environment to connect marketplace needs with innovative product development successfully.

Engineering

Engineers are the driving force behind new products and innovations in other management structures. This is most often the case in high-tech companies, in which the engineers are the most closely connected to the latest technological advances and the advantages they might offer. Companies that need to have the latest technological breakthroughs rapidly incorporated into their product lines may find this model to be very effective.

On the other hand, engineers may not be aware of or fully appreciate customer pain points and needs. They may tend to use technology because it's available and not because it actually helps the customer. This desire to use the latest gadgetry can lead to feature bloat, resulting in products with features and complexities the customer does not want or need. This adds to the costs of product development and price to the user, all of which can cause customers to go elsewhere, most likely to the simpler, less expensive option provided by the competitor.

Newer Structural Models for Innovation

Not surprisingly, organizations are experimenting with non-traditional management models as they try to improve their success at innovation. Experiment is the operative word here, as it may take some time to find the model that works best, and it will likely be customized to fit the specific industry and organizational culture. A few of these models are described here.

Fully Integrated

As the imperative nature of innovation has been more widely understood by organizational leaders, many have adopted structures in which everyone in the organization is responsible for innovation. Every individual brings a different set of observations and knowledge, and leveraging this variety of inputs is a key feature of a fully integrated model. Methodologies that allow the capture and curating of ideas and feedback are prominent in such organizations, with easy access for anyone to offer a comment or suggestion and follow-through mechanisms to review, aggregate, and assess them.

Organizations with a fully integrated structure go to great lengths to ensure each individual not only has the opportunity but also feels responsible for contributing to innovations and opportunities. They may provide dedicated time to work on ideas, either individually or in small groups. Employee goals include innovation activities that align with organizational strategies and are part of the employee's professional development. Each workforce member is accountable for creating value for customers.

IBM has invested heavily in a collection of tools, platforms, and roles to establish a strong innovation culture and discipline in which all employees are encouraged to participate. In 2008, IBM hosted an Innovation Jam in which 50,000 employees participated, offering 32,000-plus posts, and people at more than 1,000 companies serving 20 different industries contributed. This kind of commitment and support reinforces to all employees that innovation is highly important to the organization and part of their day-to-day responsibilities (Rao, Wilson, and Watkinson 2009). IBM continues to depend on its integrated structure to support an innovation ecosystem in which its research, product development, and business services divisions collaborate internally and externally (Satell 2016; 2018).

In some companies, especially large ones, the fully integrated model can become unfocused and disconnected from strategic directions. The management model in these cases will need to establish stronger communication mechanisms and tools to continue to keep strategic directions in front of personnel while capturing and leveraging inputs and feedback from them. Online databases, regular vetting of ideas, commitment of resources, and internal idea labs are just a few of the tools that have been used.

> *"One sign of whether groups are integrated is the language used to refer to different parts of the organization. When people talk about the 'editorial side' or the 'product side,' it's a giveaway that they are not one unit."*
>
> – Trei Bundrett, COO, Vox Media

Start-up Incubator

Establishing a dedicated "start-up incubator" is another popular structure for innovation. The start-up environment lends itself to rapidly moving an idea forward without the bureaucratic obstacles of a more mature organization. Mastercard, Coca-Cola, and GE, among others, have established start-up enterprises within their business organizations with goals such as building profitable new entities, becoming more agile and entrepreneurial, and identifying innovative talent (Alsever 2015). The start-up incubator can take the form of the traditional R&D lab, but it requires a broad external focus that connects with users, new technologies, and even unrelated industries, as they may hold the ideas and information needed for transformative innovation. Many organizations find that partnering with independent start-ups allows them to be more selective about which innovative solutions they will adopt and shifts risks away from the organization to the start-up. This model has the dual benefit of supporting the start-up with resources and market access it may not have otherwise.

Dual Operating System Model

Rather than rely on an existing (and likely a more traditional) operating model as the basis for innovation, consider building a dual operating system. In this blended model, the traditional system, with all its advantages for day-to-day business (e.g., process standardization and efficiency), exists in complementary fashion with a parallel and integrated innovation system. The innovation system functions as a network-based structure, similar to an internal start-up, but it functions within the established traditional operating system (Kotter 2012).

The blended model may be thought of as a dual operating system in which the innovation unit is made up of two groups of individuals (see Figure 3.1). One group—the initiative group—includes people whose responsibilities are fully dedicated to innovation. Members of the initiative group are primarily responsible for the innovation process, identifying opportunities and solutions, and transitioning those ideas through development and implementation. The second group—the subinitiative group—includes people whose responsibilities are split between the innovation group and the traditional operational system.

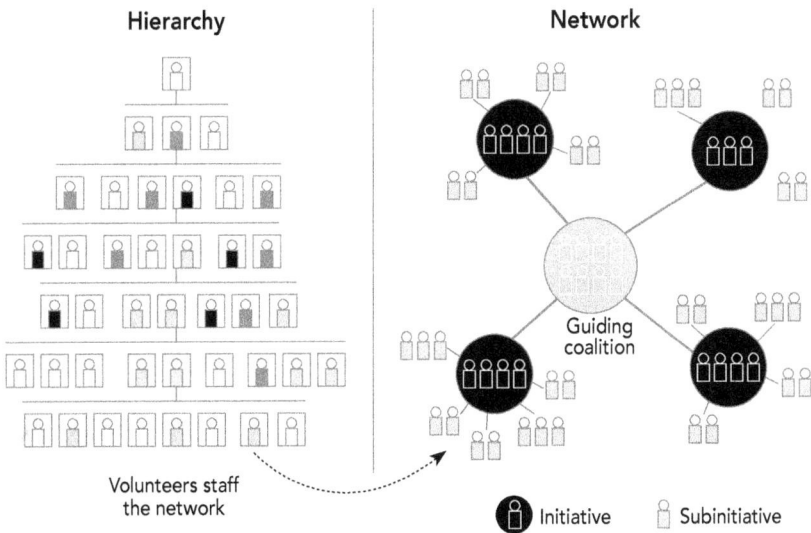

Figure 3.1 Dual operating model.   (Source: Kotter 2011; used with permission.)

Members of the subinitiative group go back and forth between the innovation unit and their home unit. This overlap allows them to bring thoughts, ideas, and feedback from their home unit for consideration, vetting, and optimization by the full innovation team (initiative group plus subinitiative group). Members of the subinitiative group also take innovation updates, prototypes, and questions back to their units. They have dual responsibilities and serve a critical role of communication between front-line employees and the innovation initiative group. A blended model can achieve effective integration between current subinitiative and forward-looking initiatives by bringing key insights to the innovation development program from operations and also by facilitating the transition of new offerings from the innovation unit to operations when they are mature enough to deploy (Kotter 2014a; 2014b).

One advantage of this system is that it can draw on employee volunteers rather than new hires. These volunteers are individuals who wish to contribute in more creative ways to new initiatives. They divide their time and serve as conduits for expertise, ideas, and feedback between their home units and the dedicated innovation team. This arrangement provides new opportunities for individual learning, skill development, and career advancement.

The dual operating system builds efficiencies into the innovation methodology and can move more quickly than the traditional system to pursue strategic solutions. New products and services, internal process innovations, and new business models can be integrated into the traditional system more efficiently due to the early and ongoing interactions between the groups. Abrupt handoffs, which are often disruptive and inefficient, are avoided. The parallel traditional system operates more effectively on day-to-day activities than the innovation system, as it was designed to do. This synergistic pairing has been shown to be highly conducive to "greater agility, speed, and creativity" for the organization's strategic changes and deployments (Kotter 2012).

Eliminate Management Structure

Most organizations continue to operate in a hierarchical fashion, even those that desire to be innovative. Given that hierarchies often lead to bureaucracy, strict division of duties, and siloing, a few brave companies have gone to hierarchy-free models in which there are few, if any, managers, and individuals are responsible and accountable for their own work.

In such an environment, the organizational structure is a peer-to-peer operating system that increases transparency, accountability, and organizational agility. The model allows businesses to distribute authority, empowering all employees to take a leadership role and make meaningful decisions. A hierarchy-free environment is more likely to allow employees to focus on outcomes and to self-organize and collaborate as needed, rather than within organizational hierarchies, functional groups, and silos. They can concentrate on the things that will improve the outcome rather than what they have been directed to do or what they believe will help themselves. Innovation then happens on its own, not because of the organizational chart or the latest internal promotion. Companies like Zappos, Valsplat, and Toyota have successfully capitalized this "holarchical" approach with outcomes-focused teams that are aligned with the company's value streams (see Appendix B, Holacracy).

Even in a hierarchy-free setting, minimal levels of management will still likely be needed. Simply identifying two levels: (1) the level that is driving organizational vision and long-term strategy; and (2) the level that is focused on execution and operations, may be all the structure needed. Keeping levels to a minimum helps to avoid the vertical siloing that occurs in many-leveled organizations (Robertson 2015).

A 2016 study by Deloitte Human Capital Trends (Deloitte 2016) found that management structures are moving away from traditional hierarchies and functional groupings to "networks of teams." Redesigning the way people work was found to be integral to employee engagement, innovation, and speed to market. Upward mobility and positional leadership are being replaced by outcomes-based performance assessments and rewards for contributions. Communication and analytic tools, open information flow, and learning centers are necessary for networks of teams to thrive. In this environment, teams come together for a purpose, then disband and reform as needed to adapt to the organization's needs (Bersin 2016). Network structures require people with strong collaborative and communication skills, which is welcome news for many employees who are not interested in strictly defined roles and limited opportunities to perform at higher levels.

WHO ARE YOUR INNOVATORS?

Finding the Right People

Managers must look for personnel who are passionate and focused but also able to shift their focus as priorities change. They must be able to move on when something doesn't pan out, quickly getting past any feelings of regret, anger, and frustration. Innovation is an exercise in learning and acting promptly on that learning. New information may drive an initiative in a new direction, and the people involved must be able to make those shifts, as well. Clinging to their favorite program or pet project will not advance innovation.

Innovative people are characterized by the ability to associate seemingly unrelated topics, ideas, and problems. They are able to connect the dots and make relevant associations because they are curious and good at asking questions, they are keen observers, they interact and experiment with the world around them, and they build strong and diverse networks (Dyer, Gregersen, and Christensen 2009). Look for people with these behaviors as you build your innovation program; they are your leaders for innovation and will serve as examples for others (see Table 3.1).

Characteristics of innovative personalities
• Curious
• Associative thinkers
• Keen observers of behaviors and activities
• Collaborators
• Experimenters
• Passionate
• Flexible
• Networkers

Table 3.1 Characteristics of innovators.

Do you need to find the next brilliant start-up genius? No, and in fact, such a search could cause you to overlook the innovative people you already have. Innovation requires a cross-section of personalities, including keen observers and artists, creative problem solvers, engineers and developers, and project managers. Every individual has skills in each of these areas, but most of us are stronger in one or two of these areas. Management's job is to identify these strengths and put them together in a way that leverages team synergies.

Innovation benefits significantly from different perspectives and peripheral areas of expertise, and looking beyond your own organization may help bring in fresh perspectives. Posting problems online and challenging anyone to help resolve them has resulted in a number of innovative solutions and will likely be quicker than limiting the effort to a smaller, internal group. Research has shown that those with the deepest knowledge of the issue are often the first to identify all the things that won't work and actually become barriers to innovation, while those with some basic knowledge but without extensive expertise are better able to see potential solutions (Thompson 2014).

You will want to balance the team based on the current stage of the innovative initiative. For example, during the early phases of an innovation initiative, double up on your creative problem solvers with less involvement from your developers and project managers—that is, less but not none. Keeping some level of input from those other areas brings a balance of perspectives and helps keep the team grounded. Similarly, as the innovation matures, don't just hand it off to engineering; keep some level of involvement from your project managers and your problem identifiers. This will help keep the solution from drifting too far from the end users' critical needs.

Keep in mind, too, that people may need some guidance and training to enhance their skills in certain aspects of innovation. Identifying not only individual gaps in experience, but also skill sets that are missing from your workforce overall, is useful to determine where to build up the expertise you need. Expanding workforce experiences with voice-of-the-customer, problem-solving, and innovation management tools, for example, may be very helpful for advancing your innovation culture.

Collaboration and Communication

People who are good at innovation are also good at collaborating and working across functions. Collaboration is an important factor in promoting teamwork, effective customer solutions, and overall innovation success. The organization's management structure can enhance collaboration by bringing in people with strong teamwork mindsets and supporting them by establishing an environment in which collaboration thrives. Facilities must be designed to encourage employee interaction and collaboration. When organizations successfully design for collaboration, they ensure the free flow of information and ideas, whether as part of a customer-service delivery workflow or day-to-day operations support. Examples include provisions for meeting areas and break areas, virtual meeting and call capabilities, as well as colocation of dependent work groups or associates (see Appendix B, Open Office). Productivity may take a hit, but that will be offset by the generation of new ideas and new enthusiasm for acting on them. Cutting-edge innovative companies such as Google have gone to great lengths to set up open office spaces, meeting rooms, and foot-traffic pathways designed to trigger chance interactions and productive collaborations (Alter 2013).

Innovative organizations welcome trial and error; innovation is a learning experience, and failing is a critical part of learning. Establishing feedback programs that allow employees to feel good about their efforts, even when they don't result as expected, sets up an environment in which people are comfortable with failure and redirections. Encouragement from management will help them keep their focus on the current priorities and applying those learnings, without feeling threatened or fearful.

Supporting employees as they innovate is a management responsibility and should be built into your organization's structure. By providing transparent and timely communications, employees always know where things stand and what their role is; this is especially true in the rapidly changing world of innovation. Encouraging and rewarding desired behaviors—from simple and informal gestures of appreciation to formal recognition and award programs—is another way to build the camaraderie and collaborative spirit that will enable the success of your innovative structure.

STRUCTURE AND STRATEGY

Structuring for innovation, however it is organized, must be tied to the organization's strategy and must adapt as the strategy changes. Keeping this in mind can help you avoid failed initiatives and innovating simply for the sake of innovating. Only if you have a clear idea of your organization's strategic direction, its current and desired competencies, and its current and desired market presence can you keep the focus on the innovation program and pipeline and organize for effective innovation.

Your organizational structure can then help you attain your strategic goals through directed innovative initiatives. For example, depending on your strategic goals, you may need to build a new division, hire staff with skill sets currently lacking in your organization, or merge units to leverage combined resources and talent. Each strategic goal is an opportunity to drive innovation toward your desired strategic outcomes, and your strategic direction will dictate your structure design.

Strategic direction drove one casket business in a new innovative direction. After more than 100 successful years manufacturing caskets, the company noted changing trends in the marketplace, specifically, the decreasing death rate and increasing rates of cremation over burial. A strategic decision was made to diversify its offerings. After analyzing the company's core competencies and available resources, it determined an acquisition program was its best option. Initially, the company planned to remain a regional company utilizing its "metal bending" expertise. Based on additional research of more than 400 acquisition targets, it settled on acquiring a business that manufactured agricultural/industrial equipment such as feeders, conveyers, and crushers. The company not only expanded its product offerings to new markets, but it also went on to acquire additional equipment manufacturers and shifted its focus beyond regional to serve a global market. This transformative strategy resulted in tripling the company's revenue in less than three years (Fairchild and Yemen 2014).

MANAGEMENT OVERSIGHT AND DECISION-MAKING MODELS

VUCA (volatility, uncertainty, complexity, and ambiguity) accurately describes the environments in which we live, work, and innovate. In fact, it is VUCA that presents many of our opportunities to innovate. An effective management structure can help to manage VUCA and corral it into an efficient innovation machine.

Such a management structure may require an overhaul of the organization's decision-making processes. Gone are the days of hierarchical, up-the-chain, down-the-chain, decision routes. These models slow decision-making, skew it toward the opinions of a select small group or individual, and introduce subjectivity and office politics into decisions.

Because innovation depends on experimenting and learning, decisions must be built into the innovation process such that experiments are designed with clear-cut objectives and measures to determine if those objectives were met. Only through experimentation, including failures, will ideas take shape and become reality. Decision-making must be objective and be able to quickly identify what is working and, perhaps more importantly, what isn't working, so appropriate changes and next-step decisions can be made.

Managers and leaders must move away from being the chief decision-makers, and employees must be prepared to take on accountability and responsibility for designing, collecting, and analyzing experimental data, then making decisions based on those data. The management structure must ensure decision-making is done at the lowest organizational level possible while still maintaining reasonable oversight.

Nathan Furr and Jeff Dyer, in their book *The Innovator's Method, Bringing Lean Startup into your Organization* (Furr and Dyer 2014), say leaders must become "chief experimenters" who focus on "forming leap-of-faith assumptions with their team, rapidly testing those assumptions through experiments (mostly with customers), and letting the data (mostly from customers) make the decisions." Highly innovative companies like Google, Amazon, and Intuit have effectively introduced these concepts in their decision-making models and organizational structures.

PUTTING IT ALL TOGETHER

The management structure that is most conducive to innovation is unique to your setting and may take time to fine-tune. Various models have been tried, as described in this chapter, and they will provide useful starting-point information. Key to success is putting good teams together—the right skill sets with the right balance at the right time. Give them the right resources and authority, in the right management structure, and they will move your organization forward with new and exciting innovations.

CHAPTER FOUR

Structuring for Product Innovation

PRODUCT INNOVATION AND STRUCTURE

"WHAT IS IT MY CUSTOMERS REALLY WANT?" is the question that should drive any organizational structure for product innovation. Product delivery models are rapidly shifting toward customized offerings, based on individual customer desires. Understanding these desires is the essential piece of successful innovation, so it follows that the organization should be structured to facilitate a thorough and deep understanding of user problems, needs, and desires. Responsibilities for gathering information on the customer perspective must be clearly assigned and coordinated. No one source, tool, or survey will tell a complete story; multiple feeds of input need to be correlated, cross-checked, and fully analyzed to find the relevant information and the best way to apply it.

Accomplishing this deep understanding of the user's needs and pain points may require shifting resources within the organization and exerting more emphasis on direct interactions with users, both current and potential. Only by getting into the customers' heads and understanding their work worlds—even better than they do—will the organization be able to offer a more attractive product, service, or business model, and stay ahead of the marketplace and the competition. This part of innovation is inherently less predictable and resistant to traditional structure and product planning approaches.

Where does responsibility for understanding customer behaviors fit in the organization? Organizations may rely on dedicated research teams, product managers, or sales and marketing staff; they may also outsource the effort to a company or individual with expertise in the methods and tools for gathering user insights. The important thing is that the structure holds some group or set of individuals responsible for the ongoing task of staying abreast of the customers' problems and needs. This information is where the organization's next opportunities will be found.

Responsibility for understanding and defining the customer's needs is unlikely to be neatly assigned to one functional group, department, or team, however. This is a cross-functional effort that draws on a variety of skills and insights, including observational and analytical. For example, a marketing department may conduct a focus group with a select group of customers. From the customer feedback received, the marketing department writes a report with their key conclusions and hands it off to the engineering department. Engineering works with marketing to create a set of specifications, then designs and manufactures the new product. From there, the product is handed off to sales, perhaps with other incremental handoffs along the way. Even in the best of circumstances, the odds of hitting a home run with this linear approach are limited.

Structuring the organization with multiple interdependencies and collaborative touchpoints offers a better approach to ensuring customer needs are central to the product offering and its development. In this way, engineering representatives would be included in the focus group. Input from multiple sources beyond the focus group would be collected across the organization, branching out to activities such as gemba exercises at customer sites, analyzing customer complaints and feedback, and researching other industries through business literature, product demos, and/or collaboration sessions. Through these collaborative activities, the potential for identifying opportunities and innovative solutions, as well as the successful development and adoption by customers, is elevated.

The extensive focus on what will not only make customers happy but also delighted, requires a full-on effort across the organization. The network structure described in Chapter 2 is an example of how structure can drive product innovation. Networked teams can approach the customer perspective from various angles and share those perspectives to stimulate innovative solutions in a way that a functional group (or series of functional groups) cannot.

UNDERSTANDING CUSTOMER NEEDS
AND HOW TO ADD VALUE

To best understand customer needs, think of the customer's situation from a process perspective—what is it they do; what steps do they currently take; what steps cause frustration, inefficiency, and/or costs; and how could those steps be reimagined to be easier for them? Now align that information with your organization's core competencies, resources, and strategic direction. The sweet spot in the middle—where the organization can innovatively solve the customers' frustrations and make their lives easier, simpler, and cheaper—is where the best innovations will arise. Alexander Osterwalder, innovation and business model consultant, refers to "pain relievers," the opportunities that address the sources of pain or frustration for the customer, and "gain creators," solutions that add value for the customer and producer (see Figure 4.1).

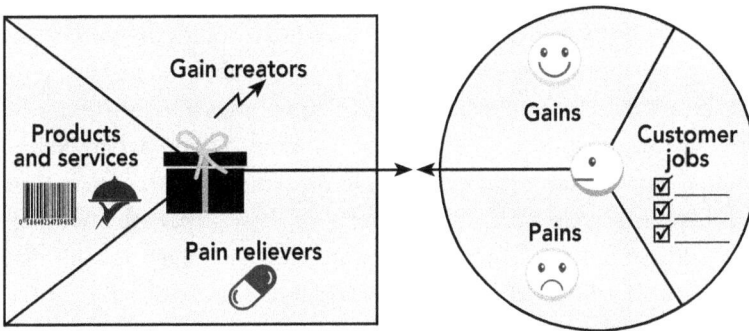

Figure 4.1 Achieving product:market fit.   (Source: Strategyzer; used with permission.)

Although tools are covered in Appendix B, a few are mentioned in more detail here because they are crucial to product innovation, and a structure for product innovation should ensure they are considered, perhaps even with dedicated customer information gathering units.

Tools such as SurveyMonkey have made the collection of customer satisfaction data simple, cheap, and fast, and this can be an excellent way to collect user feedback. Customer satisfaction data, however, are susceptible to numerous fallacies and misinterpretations that prevent effective innovation. For one thing, there is an art to asking questions that elicit useful information. Eric Ries, in *The Lean Startup* (Ries 2011), cautions against "vanity metrics," that is, asking questions that will get the answers the founder wants to hear but don't really tell you what the customers are thinking (see Appendix B, Lean Start-Up).

Be sure to ask open questions that are designed to elicit empirical information that will help make an informed decision about when opportunities exist and how best to resolve them. Evaluating survey data after the fact, without setting criteria and action thresholds before data collection, is another common misstep. Carefully designing the survey questions will allow objective interpretation and empirical decisions based on the data, which will ultimately smooth the way to a successful offering.

Getting surveys to the right audience can also be a challenge. Customers are complicated, and product purchase decisions are often separated from the actual user. If the customer relationships are through the purchasers, it may be challenging to get to the actual users for their honest opinions. Even if the actual users are responding, their answers may be influenced by many factors, including whether they're having a good or bad day, are too polite to answer honestly, or decide to provide the answer they think the surveyor wants to hear. If the timing of their experience with the product is disconnected from their responses, e.g., if they haven't used the product in a while, they may have forgotten what it was they did or didn't like about it. Also, different levels of customers may have different expectations. For one manufacturer of medical calculator software, nurses gave different responses to a series of satisfaction questions than nurse administrators and physicians—each group used the product in different ways and had different expectations. Be sure to consider all user types when researching customer desires and needs.

Fully understanding customer needs requires a range of approaches. Surveys play a role, but other, deeper methods must be employed. Objectives must be set in advance, data collected and analyzed objectively, and actions taken quickly based on what was learned from the data. Methodologies such as value analysis, design thinking, and ethnography are important tools for understanding customer needs and how to add value, and they are important considerations for designing a structure that is focused on product innovation.

Value Analysis

No organization can be all things to all customers. Understanding the value proposition is necessary to effectively select, develop, and implement innovative products and services. What is it about the solution that adds value to both sides—the customer who will use it and the provider who will make and deliver it? Of course, most situations will be more complex than this simple equation, with supply chain complexities, competing value perspectives, and economies of scale. Even in these more complex environments, however, understanding the value proposition is key to effectively meeting the user's needs, at whatever point along the product or service delivery pathway they are (Keathley 2019; Harrington and Trusko 2014). Too often, the things that get done are the things that are easy to do, and the things that are the most valuable are put off until later.

> *"Innovation is change that unlocks new value"*
>
> – Jamie Notter

In essence, value analysis is about the relative benefit to cost. The customer is looking for greater benefit (e.g., ease of use, simplicity, pain relief) and the lowest cost, while the supplier's incentive is to provide enough benefit to be attractive and add value at a cost that contributes to the organization's profit margin. Finding the point at which both criteria are met forms the core information needed to manage the innovative product's development and delivery.

According to Peep Laja, CEO of CXL, "A value proposition is a clear statement that explains how your product solves customers' problems or improves their situation (relevancy), delivers specific benefits (quantified value), [and] tells the ideal customer why they should buy from you and not from the competition (unique differentiation)" (Laja 2019). The value proposition is concise and informative; it can be used to convey the core value and objective of the innovative product to investors, senior management, innovation team members, and partners, as well as to customers. It is a useful tool to communicate and focus activities related to the innovation.

As the product development path progresses and more is learned about the product and what it offers, changes will likely be needed. The value proposition helps to keep those changes in perspective. If the value proposition is modified as the changes become evident, it will form the basis of the marketing campaign when the product is ready for launch. Keep in mind that the value proposition has at least two facets—the user's and the developer's—and possibly many more. It can be helpful to maintain different versions of the value proposition highlighting the added value from differing points of view.

> *"Value is in the eye of the beholder."*
>
> (Keathley 2014)

The most effective value propositions are accompanied by measures of value. Early on, these value measures will be estimates, but as information is gathered and more is learned about the innovative solution, value analysis becomes more accurate, allowing increasingly empirical decisions. These measures can help reduce the VUCA of innovative work (see Table 4.1).

By assigning numerical values to the benefits and costs that play into the value proposition, a value factor can be derived (see Figure 4.2). Numerous decision tools can help assign the scales and weighting for the values. A simple ratio of benefit to cost can then be assessed and used to compare different solutions to see which will provide the most value and to monitor the value proposition as it progresses and more is learned about its ability to address user pain points.

Because value analysis starts early in the innovation process and evolves with the developing product, it is integral to the team structure. Product development processes should include specified value analysis milestones, and the related expertise should be present (or easily accessible) in each team's membership. Tools that are useful in determining relative value include decision matrix, innovation portfolio, innovation maturity, and value engineering (see Appendix B).

Element of innovation	Benefit of value measures
Understand the problem or need	• Identify trends and patterns that indicate opportunities • Develop clear picture of where the problem lies
Identify problem-solving solutions	• Uncover the problem areas with biggest impacts • Evaluate relative benefits of potential solutions
Compare and prioritize alternative solutions	• Identify solution most likely to succeed • Understand benefits vs. costs of solutions
Monitor solution development	• Avoid drift away from the optimal solution • Continue to refine solution for best use experience
Deploy the solution	• Make additional value-adding refinements • Identify new opportunities
Develop organizational strategies	• Evaluate value of strategic initiatives to meet organizational excellence goals • Identify innovative solutions for key strategic challenges

Table 4.1 Benefits of measuring value. (Source: Keathley 2019; used with permission.)

Value factor = Customer benefits / Customer costs

Figure 4.2 The value factor. (Source: Keathley 2019; used with permission.)

Design Thinking

Coming up with innovative solutions to problems requires both creative and analytical thinking. Design thinking is a problem-solving methodology that draws on right-brain creative thinking and left-brain analytical thinking to bring together the pain points of the user with valuable and feasible solutions. Many problems are overly complex without apparent answers, even after some initial research and thought.

Design thinking helps to address significant and complex problem areas that involve human interactions and where historical data are limited or irrelevant, and the problem itself is not clearly defined or evident. Solutions may also be complex and must be feasible in the organizational environment, that is, cost effective and efficient.

Design thinking provides a set of tools that leverages cycles of experimentation and learning to reach a common mindset about the problem and its resolution. It provides the organization with a deep understanding of the problem, the user's pain points, and the user's perspective. The people involved in these complex problems often have differing perspectives but must reach a consensus on the best solution.

The key to design thinking is the emphasis on collaboration and synergy among the problem-solvers involved and the early establishment of a set of design criteria by which to develop and assess potential solutions to the defined problem. The design criteria form a foundation from which further idea generation and feedback analysis is accomplished. Team members have contributed and bought into the process by which the solution will be designed, evaluated, and prepared for the user. From there, solutions can be identified, tested, and assessed relative to the design criteria. Each cycle of assessments leads to learning and new design modifications.

Urban Solutions from Design Thinking

The city of Dublin, Ireland, used design thinking to address the setbacks experienced during the Great Recession in 2008.

What is?

The city's vitality had diminished and efforts to re-energize it were impeded by bureaucracy and traditional thinking. A team of city officials and interested citizens was convened to pursue a vision of revitalization that directly involved city residents, utilizing design thinking.

What if?

The team gathered data from citizens by enlisting business school students to interview people about their ideas for city improvements. This direct channel to city stakeholders resulted in more than a thousand "wishes," which were categorized in three areas: waste, water, and community. The team then held community meetings to understand more deeply the needs in these three areas. Through these sessions, the waste category shifted from trash management to wasted potential, sparking an idea to use vacant properties to experiment with revitalization projects.

What wows?

Five prototype projects were developed by the team and trialed. Feedback from residents was used to select three scalable projects: building a path to the coast, running a community center, and supporting a new business incubator.

What works?

The three projects were scaled up and implemented, resulting in improved community spirit and an experienced design-thinking team.

– (King and Liedtka 2014; Liedtka, King, and Bennett 2013)

Ethnography

Ethnography is the science of understanding human behaviors in their cultural context. Historically, ethnography has been the realm of anthropologists studying remote populations about which little was known. In more recent years, the practice of ethnography has been recognized for its usefulness in getting inside the minds of people in a particular population to understand their decisions, purchasing patterns, and sources of frustration and pain. Given the need for deep understanding of user needs to drive innovation, ethnography expands on the traditional tools used for determining customer needs. It can identify problem areas that no other method will bring to light.

As ethnographers learn about the lifestyles and behaviors in the populations they study, their notes and writings become stories about those people and their lives. These human-focused stories are rich sources of information and provide the context needed to truly understand the needs of the people. Companies such as Intuit have established formal ethnography groups in their organizations to better understand customers, their changing needs, and what solutions will be of most valuable to them.

> *"Ethnography has proved so valuable at Intel that the company now employs two dozen anthropologists and other trained ethnographers..."*
> – Ken Anderson, Intuit (Anderson 2009)

PRODUCT CHANGE MANAGEMENT

Along with the deep understanding of user needs that the organization's structure must nurture and support, a fundamental requirement for successful product innovation is a highly adaptable approach to product change management. Business disruptions may seemingly come out of nowhere, leaving the organization no choice but to adapt and adapt quickly. Disruptions may be from competitors, new technologies, climate events, financial market upsets, or global health crises. The organization that cannot adjust quickly and switch priorities on short notice will be challenged to maintain a competitive edge.

The ability to respond and adapt quickly to disruptive events requires an organizational culture that is resilient; used to frequent reassessments and pivots in directions for products, services, and business models; and unafraid to rely on trial and error in a setting of uncertainty (see Table 4.2). The network structure previously mentioned allows the interdependencies, collaborations, and decision-making authorities needed for such a culture to succeed. Maintaining this culture also relies on education and communication for members of the organization to understand the overall situation, the collective perspectives across the organization (that may differ from their own), and how they fit into the rapidly shifting environment of product and organizational changes. Developing a common terminology for describing problems and defining operational steps is also helpful (Lindborg 2020).

Features of innovative change management
• Rapid and repeated shifts in priorities and directions
• Multiple iterations of trial and error
• Network structure
• Culture of imagination, openness, and sharing
• Adequate resources, including technological
• Flexible oversight and accountability

Table 4.2 Features of innovative change management.

"You may have to fight a battle more than once to win it."

– Margaret Thatcher

Product change management benefits greatly from the introduction of fresh ideas and models that encourage associative thinking. The structure that ensures resources for learning, research, and brainstorming, as well as collaborative interactions, will enhance the capacity for imagination and be best suited for success, especially during major periods of disruption. Elements of such a structure include dedicated time for reflection and play; a culture of openness and sharing, supported by technology; a desire to find the unexpected; experimentation; and positive, hopeful attitudes (Reeves and Fuller 2020).

Managing the rapid changes of the innovative product life cycle requires flexible oversight and accountability. *Best Practices in Change Management* (Creasy et al. 2016) highlighted an alarming statistic: nearly 60% of the companies analyzed lacked the right capabilities to deliver on their change plans, while about the same percentage of companies didn't have the appropriate individuals, structures, and decision-making processes to drive the change initiatives. Furthermore, about 60% lacked the right metrics and incentives to make change efforts successful; and more than 63% of the companies faced high risks to their change efforts because of significant communication gaps between the leaders of the effort and the employees most affected by it (Voehl and Harrington 2016).

Product Life-Cycle Management

Innovative products, no matter how big a splash they make in the beginning, do not live in a vacuum, and are quickly met and surpassed by other products. Managers of the product life cycle must become adept at anticipating market changes and preparing for the next change, whether it is big or small, disruptive or sustaining. This requires constant, proactive monitoring of the product environment and regular reassessment of its value proposition. Recognizing the need for product changes in a systematic way, rather than after the competition has surpassed it and the damage is done, must be built into the organization's structure and procedures. In fact, this cycling back to the beginning of the innovation process is what sustains the innovation potential of the organization over time. These findings are inputs to the next strategic planning cycle, as well as the product life cycle.

Not surprisingly, inputs to product life-cycle management are the same things that initially drove the innovation. Again, a deep understanding of the customer's pain points will illuminate new opportunities to innovate and develop improved or new products. New opportunities and new user challenges may be driven by technology changes, major disruptive political or health events, demographic and social behavior shifts, climate and environmental changes, or the regulatory and legal environment. Holding part of the organization's structure accountable for monitoring the product environment will support new waves of innovation and organizational success.

Even with good monitoring methods in place, there will likely be periods of fluctuating success, with complicating factors such as lag times for new product adoption, unanticipated changes in the environment, or unexpected negative results from an emerging innovation. To avoid these situations and even out the overall organizational performance, many organizations develop an innovation pipeline comprising a collection of initiatives the complement each other but carry different levels of risk, time horizons, and resource needs. These initiatives will likely be on overlapping timelines, enabling efficient use of resources and ensuring new products are released on a regular and frequent basis. As one innovation matures and reaches the marketplace, another one will be in its final stages of development, while others are in the problem and/or solution identification stage (see Appendix B, Innovation Maturity).

A balanced portfolio of innovation initiatives becomes a necessary survival tactic to smooth out the volatility and uncertainty that is inherent in innovative endeavors. An innovation portfolio is useful in aligning innovative offerings based not only on their maturity but also on the organization's strategic objectives and risk acceptance. To be approved as a part of the organization's portfolio, the proposed activity needs to make better use of the resources required than if they were applied to another unfunded project. An overall balance of long-term and short-term, and disruptive and sustaining, innovations is desired. The makeup of that balance depends on the organization's tolerance for risk, its market sector, and resource availability. Small start-ups may have to rely on one high-risk product, while a large, mature organization may seek to maintain a portfolio with a designated percentage of high-, medium-, and low-risk ventures based on its own set of risk criteria (Voehl, Harrington, and Ruggles 2016; see also Appendix B, Innovation Portfolio).

Disrupting vs Sustaining Product Innovations

Much is heard about disruptive innovation, and in some people's minds, innovation equals disruption. In fact, innovation on a non-disruptive scale can be highly effective, too, and an important part of the innovation portfolio. As mentioned, the overall portfolio balance needs to include long-term and short-term product initiatives, high and low risk, and it must reflect the balance ratio that the organization has determined as optimal. Maintaining the balance helps even out risk, revenue generation, and new product releases. How can disruptive and sustaining innovations complement each other?

Sustaining innovations imitate or improve on existing products, adding incremental advancements and allowing organizations to exploit disruptive innovations from competitors by coming out with their own variation of the disruption (e.g., electronic tablets from competitors following Apple's release of the iPad). Developing and marketing sustaining innovations can help an organization stay relevant in the marketplace and remain competitive. Established providers, however, generally have the advantage in new product deployment, with a current set of loyal customers and the benefit of the inertia of current customers changing vendors. Even if a sustaining innovation offers added value over the established product, it may not be a useful approach for achieving new business growth (Christensen 1997).

Disruptive innovation introduces new business models, products, or services to the marketplace that substantially change the pre-existing environment, disrupting the status quo and driving new behaviors. The introduction of portable electronic devices, in particular the mobile phone, disrupted the communications status quo, changing human behaviors worldwide and all but eliminating prior telephony instrumentation. Disruptive innovations may not be as good as the current offering, instead providing something that is easier, more convenient, and/or less expensive. The benefits must be considered valuable and appealing for new and current customers; the value is often more about lower costs or greater convenience than about better features or utility. While disruptive innovation entails greater levels of risk, it has been shown to be the most effective approach to compete against incumbent producers (Satell 2017; Christensen 1997).

In reality, innovations fall along a spectrum from minor and incremental to radical and disruptive (Keathley 2015). Noted quality management expert W. Edwards Deming recognized the relationships and interdependencies between improvement and innovation in his "Four Prongs of Quality" model (see Figure 4.3). A structure that drives process improvement is the basis for improving existing products and service, which in turn supports process innovations (i.e., new process developments), which form the basis for innovating products and services (i.e., new value-adding products and services). Organizations need both improvement and innovation capability; these are interdependent models that need to be integrated in the organization's structure. The continuous improvement aspect of the organization's quality system is the foundation of an effective innovation management system.

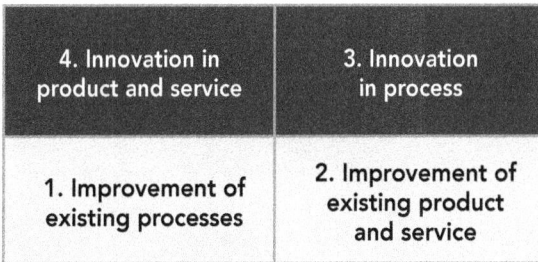

4. Innovation in product and service	3. Innovation in process
1. Improvement of existing processes	2. Improvement of existing product and service

Figure 4.3 Deming's four prongs of quality and innovation.

(Adapted from Bhalla 2010)

The "correct" balance of innovation initiatives for an organization's portfolio is based on factors such as the organization's marketplace position, the maturity of its key products, its core competencies, and the strength of its improvement system. Finding the balance and structuring the organization to achieve it can become a core competency, as shown by Corning Glass. Corning, a long-time leader in innovation, established a best practice of balancing its innovation portfolio across high- and low-risk projects. The mix is monitored over time. As projects succeed and go on to production, or fail and come off the list, new initiatives are selected from the pipeline in a way that rebalances the portfolio and maintains the desired level of risk. Corning's fiber-optics program took four years of research to identity the best solution and 20-plus years to fully develop the market. This big-risk, big-payoff program was balanced along with other less risky initiatives (Buckman and Buckman 2013; ASQ The Corning Journey).

BUILDING AN ORGANIZATION ON THE CUTTING EDGE OF PRODUCT INNOVATION

The organization that is structured to deliver a relentless focus on customers — their challenges, pain points, and concerns — will be set up for successful product (and service and business model) innovation. Collaborative structures that cross internal functions and interact with external sources are essential for the deep understanding of the customer's situation that will lead to imaginative ideas, new models, and creative solutions. Establishing expertise in the techniques that are best suited for obtaining information on customer needs should be part of the structure. A culture of flexibility and rapid adaptation rounds out the product change management picture of a structure for product innovation.

CHAPTER FIVE

Structuring for Process Innovation

WHERE IN THE ORGANIZATION DOES INNOVATION GET DONE?

IN 2018, $782 BILLION WAS INVESTED IN R&D by The Global Innovation 1000, a list of top R&D corporate spenders. Corporations from sectors such as computers and electronics, software and internet services, industrials, and automotive are represented in the top 10 most innovative companies (see Table 5.1), according to a report in Jaruzelski et al. (2018).

1. Apple
2. Amazon
3. Alphabet
4. Microsoft
5. Tesla
6. Samsung
7. Facebook
8. General Electric
9. Intel
10. Netflix

Table 5.1 Top 10 innovative organizations, 2018. (Adapted from Jaruzelski 2018)

Of note is that these companies were not the same as the top 10 companies in R&D expenditures. In fact, the top 10 innovative companies outperformed the top 10 R&D spenders on several financial metrics, including revenue growth and gross margin. How did they do this? The top 10 innovative companies were identified as having these characteristics:

- Close alignment of innovation strategy with business strategy

- A strong innovation culture with top leadership involvement

- Innovation driven by insights from end users

- Rigorous control of project selection early in the innovation process

The integration of these characteristics to create unique customer experiences that could transform their market was seen as a key success factor. These characteristics are built on internal processes that are designed for innovative outcomes.

We tend to focus on new and value-adding products, services, and business models when we talk about innovation, but internal business processes are also areas of potentially significant innovation. Methods to drive innovation are front and center across organizations that are focused on success, not a low priority to be addressed after everything else has been done. How do these organizations structure themselves to make the most of their resource expenditures toward innovative activities and outcomes? Can their practices work for other organizations?

A baseline effort for the organization is to establish its innovation methodology. This methodology must build an effective and sustainable innovation program, and the structure of the organization must go beyond merely accommodating it to prioritizing it and making it run smoothly and effectively. The innovation methodology can drive new products, services, and business models, including the development of new and better operational processes. In this chapter, we will discuss the innovation process first, then structuring for operational process innovation using the innovation methodology.

INNOVATION PROCESS—HOW DOES INNOVATION GET DONE?

"Waste is any human activity which absorbs resources but creates no value."

– James P. Womak and Daniel T. Jones
(Womak and Jones 2003)

A Common Innovation Methodology

Your organizational structure must support your expectations for innovation (i.e., build a culture for innovation) and define how innovation will get done across the organization. While it may be tempting to organize more traditionally (e.g., a "new product" division for identifying new opportunities; a business development unit for creating new markets; engineering for developing new products; and manufacturing and quality for improving processes), experience shows that this may result in "silo-ing" and difficult handoffs between those units. The "throw it over the wall" approach from department to department minimizes critical communications and information exchange, resulting in significant losses of speed and agility. Efficient use of resources and speed to delivery are key measures of successful innovation.

The innovation structure must function well in the environment of VUCA that is inherent with innovation. Innovation work is highly iterative and non-linear, and the process may be entered or exited at any point (see Figure 5.1). It is typical for the process to loop back to earlier points as information becomes available and more is known about the evolving innovation. That new information may even expose a lack of value in the innovation and result in ending its development, only to start at the beginning for the next idea in the pipeline.

If all that sounds chaotic, rest assured that without an innovation methodology, it will quickly deteriorate into even greater chaos. The methodology must keep the chaos in control without stifling energy, creativity, and speed. A higher level of tolerance for risk, failure, and confusion will be needed. Although there are many examples of innovation processes in the business literature, the primary steps are relatively consistent across them.

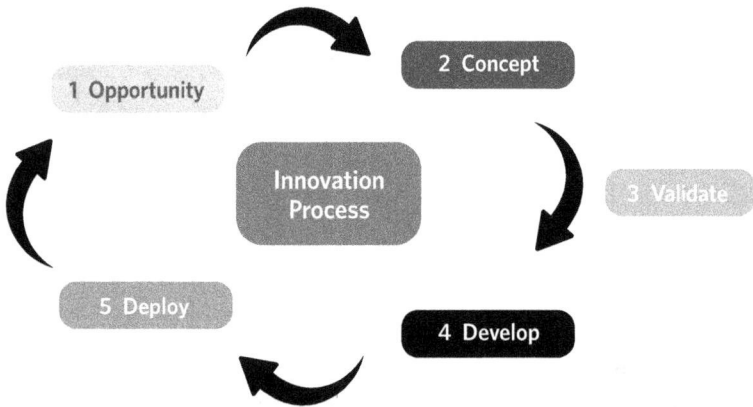

Figure 5.1 Innovation process. (Source: Peter Merrill 2020; used with permission.)

The key elements of an innovation methodology include the following:

- Begin by developing insights into the problem and identifying the opportunity.

- Follow this by researching the problem and discovering creative solutions.
    - Establish decision points and mechanisms that will keep things moving and focus resources as the solution matures.
    - Include an iterative series of steps to compare and narrow the list of solutions as you move from problem identification to optimizing the solution.

- Optimize and enhance the chosen solution to achieve the best value proposition.

- Develop the business model around which the innovation can be deployed, including manufacturing, marketing, and commercial sales, as applicable.

This is also where the cycle begins anew. The environment has changed over the time it took to develop and deploy the innovation. You have rolled out your own innovation, and others may have entered the field too, so the competitive dynamic is different. Customers and users have changed and may have different expectations. New technologies may have developed that would add value to your offerings. As more opportunities come to light, your innovation process continues to operate. In a fully functioning system, it never really stops; there is constant movement in each part of the process, with a pipeline of opportunities working their way along the process at any given time.

Taking a systematic approach to innovation is of critical importance to ensure sustainability. Different methodologies and tools may be better applied based on the phase of the process you are in (see Figure 5.1). While each of the innovation process steps, or phases, are interdependent and iterative, methodologies like design thinking are more informative in the early insight and problem research phases, while business model canvas becomes most important as the solution development phase is transitioning to the business model phase (see Appendix B).

Establishing an innovation process that is adapted to your environment and culture is a key element of structuring for successful innovation. The process needs to be understood and followed by everyone involved in your innovation program, including the workforce, suppliers, and your customers. The process also needs to be flexible, to adjust for the rapid change management essential to innovation, and it must be continuously improved as the organization shifts to accommodate new information. One way to think of the innovation process is that it serves as the operating system (OS) of the organization that supports multiple innovation initiatives, similar to a smartphone's OS that supports multiple apps. The best organizational structure will be the one that allows the innovation methodology to flourish.

Some role-model best practices of structuring for innovation include:

- Innovation ecosystem and innovation catalysts (Intuit): This employee-centered network provides innovation mentoring, resources, and skill development, including assistance with design thinking, understanding customer pain points, and prototyping (Martin 2011).

- Expert acceleration sessions (Kimberly-Clark): These one-day sessions bring outside innovation thought leaders in to meet with business teams to challenge current thinking and create new strategies (Uphill 2016).

- i-mentors (Whirlpool): Innovation mentors share their knowledge of innovation methodology, tools, and mindset, and provide guidance to business teams that are focused on resolving challenging business situations (Poosen and Nakagawa 2008).

Quality System as a Catalyst for Innovation

As noted in Chapter 4, W. Edwards Deming recognized the interdependencies between quality and innovation (see Figure 4.3). He said that innovation requires well-established processes and successful products and services, which are driven by a robust quality system and a culture of continuous improvement. Only when this system is working smoothly can new elements be brought in to innovate processes, then products and services, enhancing their value for customers, employees, and stakeholders, including society at large. The continuous improvement aspects of our quality systems form the bedrock for innovation.

Look to your business planning and performance excellence system for the key skills and expertise to establish your innovation structure. A recent ASQ/Forbes study of 2,291 executives and managers showed that self-described world-class companies are more likely overall to cite strong quality programs as a vital tool to drive innovation. Managing business risks and continuously learning and improving are core to quality systems. In fact, a key change in the most recent update to the ISO 9001 Quality Management System (QMS) standard is the increased focus on risk-based thinking (ISO 9001:2015 standard). This change was made to help organizations address risks and opportunities in a structured manner. These QMS elements enable an organization to tune in to customers more readily, identify and appropriately control risks, and recover quickly from failure—all essential to the innovation structure.

ISO 56002, Innovation management — Innovation management system — Guidance, published in July 2019, is the first in the 56000 Innovation Management System series (Forbes 2014). It is modeled on the ISO 9001 quality standard and supports the integration of the innovation management system into an existing QMS. The standard provides useful guidance on innovation leadership, planning, support, and operations, as well as monitoring and improving your innovation methodology. Clause 8 describes the criteria for innovation processes; it includes the identification of opportunities, creation and subsequent validation of concepts, and development and deployment of solutions. Innovation structure in the standard is described by initiative, which may be a single business unit, multiple units, or collaboration across a range of external entities, e.g., suppliers, customers, and academia. The standard notes that the structure may change over time as the initiative progresses and points out that a loose structure may be adopted, e.g., crowdsourcing (Merrill 2019).

Organizing the Workforce around Your Innovation Process

The organizational structure around which you execute the innovation process must incorporate cross-functional employees who can contribute their varying perspectives and sources of insights. Insular thinking is unlikely to give you the fresh ideas you need to be innovative. Matrix organizations and external partnerships that bring together creative thinkers with process engineers, designers with users, and problem solvers with marketers can jump-start the innovation program and must be driven by the organization's structure and process.

Flat organizational structures, as described in Chapter 3, tend to be better for innovation, in part because they don't get bogged down by layers of decision-makers and irrelevant decision factors. Allow decision-making at the lowest level possible, based on well-thought-out criteria that support a go/no-go decision to move to the next step. Flat structures and clear decision-making policies will provide the speed and agility needed to excel at innovation.

The organizational structure for innovation cannot operate in a vacuum or independently of the rest of the organization. There are top-down and bottom-up aspects to innovation, and the structure must facilitate both. The top-down aspects include leadership setting the expectations for innovation and building a strategy that clearly shows the direction and the end goals of the organization. Bottom-up structures support the capture and free flow of insights and ideas from front-line employees and others into the innovation process.

STRUCTURES THAT DRIVE PROCESS INNOVATION

With a common approach to innovation in place, how can the organization use that approach to create or renew business processes?

Understand Key Business Processes

Start by mapping key processes and showing the interfaces among them, as well as the responsible organizational areas (e.g., customer service, marketing, production, etc.) Map them from the customer's perspective (see Appendix B, Service Blueprinting). Identify where issues exist; these problem areas become your best opportunities to make innovative changes to your processes. They will highlight structural changes that can leverage your strengths and competencies while improving the interfaces and decision pathways needed for high-functioning processes. For example, are you experiencing delays in market releases? Looking at your business process map, identify the places where the delays are occurring and consider what new information could be brought to innovatively address them. Perhaps a new definition or a reassignment of responsibilities could streamline decisions and speed things up. Automation is another common, and often successful, approach to process innovation. The key is to follow your innovation methodology to identify issues and opportunities, creatively research solutions, develop the best solution and implement it.

Keep Up-to-Date on New Information

Proactive identification of changes in the business environment, including new technologies, must be a component of your structure. This should be an assigned responsibility with committed resources, high prioritization and visibility, and defined expectations. It should not be in the "as you have time" category of multiple other responsibilities for groups such as your executive management team, the quality organization, or product engineering. One large medical device company hired a senior vice president for medicine and technology to serve as an international scout. This high-level role was tasked with scouring the planet for new technologies that could drive the product line to the next generation. This was not done by finding new technologies and lobbing them over to another group to develop. Rather, the structure was based on a network of:

1. Internal stakeholders, such as R&D and operations

2. Small businesses with partner relationships to the organization

3. External sources of knowledge and expertise, such as universities and large technology companies

The mission of the senior vice president was to "keep the organization's sights set on the future so they are not ignoring what is coming." This key role should be in charge of the KMS, as well, thereby ensuring the information collected is widely distributed to other groups and individuals who can use it to be innovative. An effective KMS is one of the most important assets an organization can have (Appendix B, Knowledge Management System).

Besides staying on top of new technologies, maintaining a strong structure for innovation requires methodologies for staying in close touch with your customers and potential customers (see Chapter 4). Keep in mind who the users are when process innovation is your aim. They will be the process suppliers, the process owners and operators, and the process output recipients, and it is their pain points in the process that need to be addressed. Understanding process users' needs may expose opportunities for creative solutions that lead to better safety, smoother handoffs, and greater efficiencies. These solutions may be structural in nature, e.g., geographic placements and the need for more or less colocation or the implementation of new technologies to support remote teams.

Design Thinking for Process Innovation

Design thinking (see Appendix B) helped one hospital reduce its ER wait times and add millions of revenue dollars. After employees received training in design thinking (through the HHS Ignite program), they set about solving the issue of patients in the ER with less urgent health issues who endured such long wait times that they often left without being seen. After trialing several possible options, including a kiosk to direct patients, they refined the solution to a new check-in desk where a clinician (nurse or EMT) directs patients very quickly to the most appropriate setting for their healthcare need, be it the ER, a clinic, the pharmacy, or some other area of the hospital.

– (Liedtka, Azer, and Salzman 2017)

Process Improvement Upgraded for Innovation

Quality engineers are often the drivers of process improvement, utilizing tried-and-true methods such as lean and Six Sigma. These problem-solving approaches, along with other related tools such as Design for Six Sigma, TRIZ, and FAST, can be helpful in identifying process problem areas and designing innovative solutions. Each of these tools is described in Appendix B.

Focusing proactively on unmet user needs, versus fixing current problems, distinguishes the use of these tools when applied for innovation. In a traditional organizational structure, they may be used in an isolated quality improvement effort, where access to necessary information and resources that are needed for evaluation and deployment can limit their usefulness for process innovations. A network structure, specifically a horizontal process structure (see Chapter 2) or a dual operating system (see Chapter 3), is more likely to be successful.

Risk Tolerance for Innovation

Risk is inherent in the innovation process. At every step, risk must be analyzed, and appropriate adjustments must be made. Risk tolerance is greater in the early stages of an innovation; as a solution emerges and enters development, the need to reduce risks will increase. The organization's structure must acknowledge this and allow the flexibility in risk acceptance that is needed for successful innovation of business processes, as well as for products and services.

Risk is best analyzed with relevant, objective data. Taking time to assemble key process performance data will save time later by avoiding bad decisions and having to redo development efforts. Look at the process outcomes and determine how you can evaluate their level of success — then look at those measures over an appropriate amount of time to establish a true understanding of how well the process is working. Be careful not to rely on measures that are simply easy to collect or that reinforce preconceived assumptions.

With the results of your risk measures, use a decision matrix tool to compare options and prioritize areas to address first for the biggest impact (see Appendix B, Decision Matrix). Your risk-based decision model will be most effective if it is integrated into all aspects of the innovation methodology, from early idea vetting through narrowing down options, development decisions, and deployment. The risk model will change; stay on top of the risk profile and regularly adjust actions and priorities.

Most risk management programs are intended to narrow variability and reduce the chances of something going wrong. While this objective is very important in many settings, *when it comes to innovation, higher risks lead to bigger payoffs;* you are looking for a big win and radical solutions. With this in mind, look at risk assessment as a source of opportunities. Tolerance limits need to be wide, especially in the early stages of defining and developing an innovative process change. Risk management exercises are also necessary for managing your innovation pipeline and keeping your desired balance of innovation initiatives in place (see Chapter 4). Without a well-honed risk management process, you may proceed down a path with risks that are either too high or too low. Either case can lead to limited success and delays as you redirect.

Data Analytics

The term "big data" refers to the huge sets of data enabled by constantly advancing technology. Big data takes many forms, and it presents with varying degrees of quality. It changes frequently and rapidly. Big data is a reality of our current times; it presents great challenges but also great opportunities for innovation. Analyses of all these data are essential for rapidly addressing the large, complex, and unstructured problems we face. Organizations must factor the incorporation of big data analytics into their innovation programs.

Many tools are already available for the analysis of big data, with new tools presenting every day. For example, Amazon Web Services provides a suite of tools for data analytics (aws.Amazon.com). Data analytics can boost an organization's ability to inform innovative solutions and speed their delivery. For best results, it must be based on sound quality principles and innovation methodologies, and it should be used only when it can provide information that simpler process improvement tools and statistical analyses cannot.

From an organizational perspective, effective data analysis requires cross-functional teams and the involvement of subject matter experts (SMEs). As noted elsewhere, networked organizational models tend to be more effective at driving these cross-functional interactions, with the benefit of bringing multiple perspectives into play and stimulating creative thinking. SMEs are needed to provide context for the data, the theory behind the analytical process, and the perspective for potential solutions derived from the analysis (Snee, DeVeaux, and Hoerl 2014).

These cross-functional teams may become a separate part of an organization's structure. Alphabet, the parent company of Google, established its "X" enterprise as a "think tank-like" initiative where SMEs from multiple backgrounds are tasked with investigating what might be considered the absurd. Questions such as "Should we build houses on the ocean?" and "Are space elevators feasible?" are advanced to better understand major problems, such as housing shortages. The questions are posed and explored, using cross-functional brainstorming, rapid evaluation methods, prototypes, etc. Crucial modern-day problems are investigated, and no idea is too extreme for consideration. The objective is to find radical solutions using feasible technology, with the long-term goal of creating new world-changing organizations (Thompson 2017).

How might the organization use data analytics for innovation? Understanding forecasts and making predictions may help to determine the feasibility of certain solutions. Classification of objective data may help identify priorities within a set of data points. Pattern identification and detection of anomalies may help identify problem areas or opportunities for efficiencies. Data analyses can help understand the data themselves and find ways to better navigate them for useful information.

We are swimming in data, with huge volumes being collected constantly. Finding the most useful or helpful data points would be impossible without, well, without data analyses that can reduce the data to their most significant elements (Radziwill n.d.). In fact, an important step in data analytics, done with the aid of those SMEs, is to structure the unstructured data in a way that helps define the problem and establish metrics for assessing further analysis and development (DiBenedetto, Hoerl, and Snee 2014).

Given the variety of data sources and the potential for lack of control over the collection of diverse data, data analyses also need to determine the quality of data being analyzed. The adage of "garbage in, garbage out" applies as much as ever for big data analytics. Understanding the validity of the data under analysis is a necessary part of understanding the accuracy and reliability of the analytical outcomes.

The organization's structure can address the use of big data in its processes by ensuring the accessibility of teams to data sources and by providing the tools, both traditional and cutting edge, to enable big data analyses. Approaching these activities with tried-and-true quality principles in mind — things like consistent processes, empirical objectives, checks and tests, and validation exercises — will ensure big data works in the organization's best interests.

Building an Agile Organization

Change management and decision-making can quickly bog down the organization's processes if not carefully defined and implemented. Speed and agility require rapid decisions based on objective criteria and data, not on bureaucratic decision trees that may take days to conclude, nor on impulsive reactions from a key individual. Establishing a structure that drives these data analyses and rapid decisions, e.g., flat hierarchy, networks of teams, analytical tools, and expertise, will prepare the organization for those inevitable business disruptions, allowing it to respond quickly and effectively. The more visionary the organization is (or wishes to be), the more important it is to have an environment of organizational agility (Lyke-Ho-Gland 2016).

Agile organizations systematically work to identify opportunities and evaluate risks, and they are also adept at planning and executing solutions to address their opportunities, within their risk tolerance boundaries. During the COVID-19 pandemic, organizations were forced to respond with agility and quickly act on the challenges and opportunities they faced; for some, turning to their core practices for data analysis and artificial intelligence enabled them to rapidly and effectively address significant disruptions (see Table 5.2). Success factors for agile organizations include:

- Alignment of analytics with organization strategy and business priorities

- Culture of cross-functional teamwork and learning cycles

- Front-line workers authorized to make data-driven decisions

- High tolerance for ambiguity

Aligning decision policies with organizational strategy is important for directional progress leading to organizational success. Effective business processes ensure clear decision criteria are in place, frequent decision points are built in, and all actions are aligned with organizational priorities and strategies. One such model is lean start-up (LSU); in this model, the process from early idea to commercial readiness is streamlined by using empiric data to test the value proposition, first, of the most basic solution offering, or minimum viable product (MVP), and then in successive cycles of solution development (Ries 2011; see Appendix B, Lean Start-Up).

Critical challenge area	Rapid response
Employee protection and support	• More accurate prediction of employee availability and need for contingency measures • Workforce management tool MVP—three weeks
Strategic and financial decisions	• Gain insights into changing commodity prices and inflation rates within minutes • Finance tool MVP—three weeks
Supply chain	• Ramp-up of critical inventory levels based on improved forecasting • Supply chain end-to-end visibility tool MVP—three weeks
Customer engagement	• Optimize marketing and sales targets by improving personalized messaging and modification of product offerings • Customer-centric analysis tool MVP—two weeks

Table 5.2 Agility and data analytics in response to pandemic (MVP = minimum viable product).

(Adapted from Henke, Puri, and Saleh 2020)

Other structures that lend themselves to agility are parallel processes such as scrum and colocation of design and manufacturing. Parallel processing requires interactions across the stages of development, so learning is immediately fed into the cycle and addressed rather than waiting until development is finished or nearly done. The scrum model, a subset of the agile methodology, uses concurrent development and testing in short, iterative cycles, allowing test results to immediately inform continuing product development.

Colocating key functions is another way to improve communication and interactions, allowing them to address issues in real time, not days, weeks, or months later. Under Armour found that bringing designers and manufacturers together under the same roof not only facilitates efficiency and speed to market for its athletic clothing, but it also allows rapid adaptations based on early customer evaluations, reducing the risk of manufacturing large runs of new styles that don't do well in the marketplace (Halzack 2017).

Parallel processes and colocation are structural approaches that can add efficiency to the organization's process structure — a critical reality given the speed with which innovation occurs. Once the innovative solution is in development, any time lost in getting to deployment lowers the probability of a successful rollout. Competitors may beat you to the marketplace; newer technologies or user preferences may have already come and gone, leaving you with an outdated solution; and/or you may have lost organizational competencies through attrition of key personnel and other resource constraints.

TECHNOLOGY

While innovation is often equated (incorrectly) with technological advancements, there is no doubt that technology drives innovative changes to business models and processes. Technology must be accounted for in the organizational structure such that technological developments are leveraged into new offerings and business models. This does not mean jumping on every new application or device that comes along; rather, staying current with technology and strategically assessing which technologies can be helpful and how they can be implemented is necessary. The organization's structure must be designed for effective assessment and use of technology.

Automation is a frequent driver of process innovation; it not only introduces efficiencies in processing, but it also frees up employees to focus on other aspects of innovation. Automation is necessary to effectively carry out complex processes and manage complex systems (and to remain competitive, in most industries). Organizations that fall behind with technology and automation soon become endangered.

Automated systems are increasingly able to learn and self-adjust, and "some enterprises have started using intelligent automation to drive a new, more productive relationship between people and machines" (Wells and Kralj 2016). The cost justification for using automation should be focused on enhancing the skills of the workforce and redirecting their contributions to those innovative activities that require human thinking and brain power. Understanding how customers access and use products and services also must be factored into technology and automation assessments (see Chapter 7).

Collaborating with suppliers is another potentially rich source of technological innovation. Advancements in technology have enhanced order fulfillment processes through more accurate inventory management and robotic tools. Tracking of shipments and deliveries, whether from the supplier to the manufacturer, or from the manufacturer to the customer, is more precise, secure, and readily available, all due to technology. The use of improved sensor technology allows better control of sensitive shipments (Day 2020). The Industrial Internet of Things (IIoT) brings these various technologies together, providing rich sources of information from which opportunities for process innovations can be mined. In the automotive industry, for example, the IIoT has led to significant production efficiency gains, and in a near reversal of Henry Ford's innovative assembly-line concept that efficiently cranked out identical black cars, the IIoT has enhanced capabilities for the individual customizations that are increasingly requested by car buyers (Masters 2017).

Communication technology needs to keep pace with the organizational structure and environment. Within the structure, open communication is essential for effective process innovation. Exchange of ideas, insights, task information, and decisions, between workers, customers, and external partners, must occur freely and quickly, and there are many technologies available to assist (see Appendix B, Open Innovation). Key requirements of communication technology include supporting formal and informal channels, easily accessible but with appropriate security, and always available. Increasingly, coworkers are not colocated, and their ability to communicate must not be hampered by technological barriers. Systems such as texting, social media, online collaboration tools, and video/teleconferencing services complement phone and email technologies and can enable the information sharing that is so critical for innovation.

Given the pace of change in the technology world, an organization's structure needs to include systematic monitoring of new developments and disruptive technologies such as virtual reality, machine learning, new energy sources, and biomechanical interfaces. One of these cutting-edge technologies may be the source of your next process innovation.

SUSTAINING YOUR BUSINESS PROCESSES FOR INNOVATION

> *"Learning and innovation go hand in hand. The arrogance of success is to think that what you did yesterday will be sufficient for tomorrow."*
>
> – William Pollard

The key to maintaining your organization's structure for innovation is learning. William Pollard was a 19th century Quaker clergyman who realized that innovation is dependent on accepting that needs and opportunities constantly evolve, and that innovative thinking is always needed to continue addressing them. So, the idea of innovation is not new, but we are often resistant to making it happen. Learning requires open and honest feedback, and organizational culture can inhibit it. Failures and mistakes often expose innovations, but if people are not comfortable with owning mistakes and discussing them openly, no learning can be done.

When Alan Mulally took over the reins at Ford Motor Company, he was charged with turning around a failing company. His team of direct reports, approximately 12 of them, all highly placed senior executives, showed up for their weekly status meetings with Mulally, business scorecards in hand, and reported "all systems go" with all metric indicators in green. He challenged them and asked why the company's performance was suffering if everything was good. There wasn't much of an answer, but after a few weeks of this, one brave department head came to the meeting with one indicator in yellow. This led to open discussion about the issue and the realization by the group that this open dialog was welcome and encouraged by the new CEO. Soon, multicolored scorecards were the norm, problems began to be solved, and the company's performed was turned around (Jane Keathley, personal communication, World Conference on Quality and Improvement 2010, St. Louis, MO).

Why is it so hard to hold lessons learned meetings at the end of projects? Many organizations include these in their plans, but, in reality, they may be postponed for so long that no one can remember the lessons, or they may be canceled altogether because of competing priorities and limited time. The organization must develop the discipline to formally capture the problems, solutions, and improvements promptly and convert them into changes for future efforts. Consider keeping a shared log or spreadsheet that is updated on a regular (e.g., weekly) basis to collect current and recent activities, problems that came up, and potential solutions. Then, at the end of the project, there is already a list of lessons learned that just takes a few minutes to review and distill into information to be added to the KMS (see Appendix B, Knowledge Management System). All individuals engaged in the innovation should maintain a project notebook; these notes are frequently used to back up patent applications and collect best practice knowledge. A successful innovation structure depends on learning cycles and applying those lessons.

INNOVATION PROCESS FOR PROCESS INNOVATION

Building a structure for process innovation leads to new and better processes and ultimately to successful product and business model innovations. Lines of management and communication must clearly identify who is responsible for which aspects of innovation and how the interactions among them will be managed. Alignment with strategy will ensure that key processes move the organization in the desired innovative direction. A common innovation methodology supports efficient communications and activities, reducing wasted time and misuse of resources, and helping to rally the workforce around the innovation initiatives. The continuous improvement models (e.g., lean, Six Sigma, DFSS, FAST) of your quality system form a solid basis for process innovation, providing a baseline of tools, concepts, and expertise. Newer tools and technologies are also available, such as data analytics, robotics and machine learning, and the IIoT. Focusing the structure for process innovation on understanding critical needs, managing risk, and maintaining flexibility and agility are key to the long-term success of your program.

CHAPTER SIX

Structuring for Sales and Marketing Innovation

CONNECTING SALES AND MARKETING WITH INNOVATION

"It's not about having the right opportunities. It's about handling the opportunities right."

– Mark Hunter, CSP; Author, *High Profit Prospecting*

The sales and marketing functions of the organization play their most significant roles in innovation through their interfaces with customers. Sales and marketing employees are usually closest to the customer and in the best position to listen to them and observe firsthand their situations, problems, and pain points. Well-developed customer relationships engage customers and make them feel comfortable conveying the things they like and the things that cause issues for them. Sales and marketing personnel are therefore at the front line in finding and learning about innovation opportunities. Organizational structures that highlight these relationships and emphasize the importance of the customer's perspective lead to successful innovation.

The innovative challenges related to sales and marketing are as great, if not greater, than those presented to product development and engineering. Cars in the same price range and classification are approximately the same brand to brand. You have a hard time telling one car from the next, but each advertisement needs to be different, creative, innovative, and informative. There is no greater innovative challenge than preparing an advertisement that runs for 30 seconds during the Super Bowl that will convince viewers that they should buy your car over all the cars. Many good products have been complete failures due to poor promotional campaigns. Likewise, many poor products have been successful due to excellent promotional campaigns.

Most people in their preconceived mind know what roles the marketing and sales departments play; however, these roles vary from organization to organization. We have used the following definitions of the roles in this book:

Marketing: Manages processes through which goods and services move from concept to the customer. It includes the coordination of four elements called the four P's of marketing:

1. Identification, selection, and development of a product

2. Determination of its price

3. Selection of a distribution channel to reach the customer's place

4. Development and implementation of a promotional strategy. This includes designing and approving packaging design.

Sales: The function of a sales department is to engage in a variety of activities with the objective to promote the customer purchase of a product or the client engagement of a service, according to the American Marketing Association. Some business management professionals consider sales an outgrowth of the marketing function, but others consider it an independent aspect of an enterprise's overall operational scheme, also according to the American Marketing Association.

In many industries, sales structures are based on personal interactions and in-person visits to establish a relationship that leads to a purchase of goods or services. This relationship allows the salesperson to observe up close what the customer deals with during their work. These observations are invaluable in understanding pain points, problems, and the opportunities they present (see Appendix B, Ethnography). Sales structures that are good for innovation enable these interactions, for example, by providing interactive sales tools or by including observation skills and techniques in sales staff training. The sales structure can contribute significantly to the collection of customer and marketplace data to feed into the innovation cycle, and the structure should recognize and leverage this important source of input for innovation (see Figure 6.1, Sales structure for innovation).

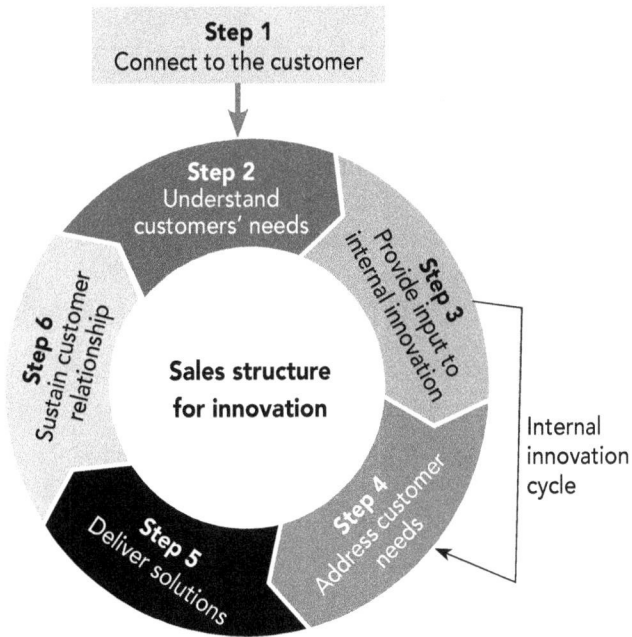

Figure 6.1   Sales structure for innovation.

(Adapted from Spotio 2018; used with permission.)

Similarly, organizing the marketing function to constantly screen for new markets, changes in customer/industry patterns and behaviors, and new customer relationship tools will bring in a steady source of insights that can lead to new opportunities or potential solutions for previously identified problems. Proactive research into customer adoption patterns by the marketing organization helps to project business trends and identify customer support needs. The marketing function needs to interact not only with the sales function but also with the organization's strategy planning and product development functions, and the organization's structure needs to enable these touchpoints.

Because marketing employees are in close contact with the external customer/consumer, they are well-positioned to start the first step in the innovation cycle—opportunity recognition. New products and services should be triggered as a result of market-driven specifications or value propositions (see Chapter 4, Value Analysis). The market specification may be developed as a result of marketing relationships with customers and a thorough understanding of the customers' present and future needs, or as a result of an inquiry from product development to determine the feasibility of developing a specific new product or service. In any case, the market specification defines the expected value addition of the opportunity and serves as the foundation and system requirements for the new product development cycle. Future evaluations of the potential of a new product or service should be compared against the original market specification plus any additional new information.

Information that is gained by sales and marketing must be conveyed to the rest of the organization if it is to be leveraged and put to constructive use. This may be as simple as sending an email to the product manager or other key individual, or entering the information into the KMS, but more likely the information will need to be explained, discussed, and analyzed to reach decisions on feasibility and next steps. Including sales and marketing representatives on innovation teams is one way to ensure the necessary handoffs of information from customer to solution development. Make sure all sales and marketing staff understand their responsibilities for bringing observations and information about customer needs and issues to the table for innovative problem solving. Add the responsibility to job descriptions. Task executive and senior management with ensuring it happens. Determine your processes for vetting this feedback for ideas worth pursuing further.

When innovations are deployed, the sales and marketing employees play key roles in helping customers understand and adopt them. No matter how good the innovative offering is, there will be a period of adoption as users understand how to benefit from it. This adoption period will vary depending on the nature of the new offering and on the individual customer's situation; sales and marketing employees are essential in helping with this adoption by publicizing the value proposition early on, providing useful training and guideline materials, and ensuring a support network with readily available answers to questions from new users. Customers may require individualized assistance with the adoption of new offerings. For example, in the contract clinical research industry, sales teams focus on the unique value the contract research organization (CRO) can bring to the drug or device sponsor. This unique value will depend on the nature of the sponsor (e.g., large pharma, mid-size device manufacturer, start-up biotech, etc.) and the types of efficiencies the CRO can provide to the sponsor (e.g., relevant therapeutic expertise; single, global clinical database). The ability to innovatively customize the research approach for the sponsor, and then guide the sponsor through that unique value proposition, is perhaps the single most important factor in CRO business development (Jane Keathley, personal communication with Carolyn Maki, Senior Executive, Pharmaceutical Business Development).

The value proposition should be evident from the beginning of the development cycle, not created when the solution is ready for the marketplace. Defining the value proposition early in the solution development cycle and refining it as new information is learned during development results in a well-honed message and fewer delays in reaching the marketplace. Advertising, sales materials, and marketing events are driven by the value proposition. Including sales and marketing throughout the cycle helps to ensure a robust value proposition is available at this stage and requires a structure that readily brings these teams together.

The biggest market successes result from innovative business models, and marketing plays a key role. Determining the best marketing approach, that is, how you position the product and make it so attractive as to be irresistible to the customer, can make or break a rollout. This requires the in-depth understanding of and engagement with the customer that the sales and marketing groups can provide. As told by Furr and Dyer (2014), a new drug for depression with the same mechanism of action as the leading depression treatment was launched a few years ago, only to experience low sales. Upon interviewing customers (both physicians and patients), the company discovered that a competitor's drug was so strongly associated with depression treatment that alternatives were not being considered by prescribing physicians and patients. By changing its marketing program to focus on "anxiety" treatment, the company was able to successfully drive increases in sales. Other successful business model innovations include: the shift in the IT world from hardware to services (e.g., IBM, Apple); the transition in the retail world from storefronts to online sales (e.g., Walmart, Warby Parker); and digital disruptors of traditional service models (e.g., Airbnb, Uber, Netflix). Business model changes such as these are more likely to revolutionize a business than a next-generation product or more customer-friendly service program.

Rewards and incentives may also be useful for connecting sales and marketing to innovation. Reinforcement of sales and marketing practices that are conducive to innovation may take the form of compensation structures that move away from sales volumes and instead reward behaviors that result in open and informative customer relationships. Incentives based on customer satisfaction and number of new ideas may be helpful. Scaling commissions to reward the rollout of new and innovative offerings can encourage sales and marketing employees to work through the challenges of the customer learning and adoption curve.

SALES AND MARKETING ORGANIZATIONAL CHARTS

Organizing the sales and marketing functions with a structure that encourages and even drives innovation must be customer focused. A 2016 Deloitte study found that "...only 26% of large companies (more than 5,000 employees) are functionally organized today (i.e., sales, marketing, finance, engineering, service, etc.), and 82% are either currently reorganizing, plan to reorganize, or have recently reorganized to be more responsive to customer needs" (Bersin 2016). Overall, "92% of the companies...surveyed cited 'redesigning the way we work' as one of their key challenges, making this the #1 trend of the year."

What is driving this need to reorganize? As described in Chapter 2, traditional models of organizational structure, based on functional areas, are not meeting the needs of the workforce or the organization in today's environment of innovation. Information technology and instant communications have led to a shift from traditional functional and hierarchical models to network-based models. Networks involve clusters (or nodes) and path lengths (see Appendix B, Organization Network Analysis). Clusters are akin to silos and represent functional groups; these groups are important to a well-functioning organization in that the individuals in them need to work closely and collaboratively. Path lengths reflect the distance between clusters. They may be related to physical distance or cultural/social differences, but the greater the path lengths, the more likely the clusters will be isolated. In many organizations, the path length between sales and marketing and other functional areas is long, perhaps due to sales and marketing employees being distributed widely across geographical areas and/or frequently traveling to customers or because of differences between the sales and marketing cultures relative to other functional areas. Effective innovation requires shortening the path lengths as much as possible to encourage interactions between clusters, sharing of knowledge, and effective communications.

NETWORK TEAMS

Relaxing the structure around the clusters or functional groups to allow more fluidity in team makeup is a potential model for enhancing innovation. General Stanley McChrystal used this model effectively during the Iraq war, as told in his book, *Team of Teams* (McChrystal et al. 2015; McDowell et al. 2016). McChrystal "created a new structure that allowed for dynamism and flexibility within the overall (military) organizational structure." The new structure was needed to counter the adaptable, networked structure of the Al Qaeda foe. The traditional hierarchical military structure was not working in the rapidly shifting and unpredictable battle environment.

Teamwork has long been a staple of organizational values and structure models. The dynamics of successful teams include trust, purpose, and adaptability. They work because they are small and intimate; team members know each other, and communication is quick and effective. These advantages do not scale well in larger, more complex organizational structures, however. The teams become siloed, trust breaks down across teams, and inefficiencies develop.

In a network of teams model, the trust, purpose, and adaptability that characterize small teams are established across individual teams. Roles, responsibilities, and professional career paths change frequently, and the team makeup is very fluid. Individuals transition in and out as needed. The interactions between teams become the responsibility of representative individuals, not the entire team. These contact points are where trust and efficiencies are built across teams and are the conduits for rapid changes when needed.

A network of teams empowers the teams to make decisions. Information is centralized, with real-time accurate data available for sound decisions. Learning, the essential element of innovation, becomes embedded in the structure. Leadership and creativity skills are critical for every job role, not just the top levels. Performance reviews and reward programs are based on teamwork and contributions to the organization's shared objectives more than individual performance.

Organizing the sales and marketing group to embed them within these network teams allows them to bring their unique, qualified perspectives to the innovation effort and contribute their expertise in ways that staying in a siloed functional unit cannot. The model is increasingly being adopted in government and business, in sectors such as healthcare (Cleveland Clinic) and manufacturing (3M). Improvements in organizational outcomes, including customer satisfaction and time to output/delivery, have resulted (McDowell et al. 2016).

> "We have to think of companies like Hollywood movies—people come together and bring their skills and abilities to projects and programs, they build and deliver the solution, and then many of them move on to the next movie later."
>
> – Josh Bersin

Organizations that opt to retain the functional hierarchical structure for sales and marketing are likely to be large companies with many employees. In situations where greater control is desired, traditional models work best. Inherent in a control model is limited flexibility, which is not associated with innovation. However, Apple, which is generally considered a highly innovative company, is structured with a hierarchical organization, with functional areas designated at the senior leader level and product areas designated at the lower levels (Meyer 2019b). Apple's organizational chart is not the usual top-down model, however; it is set up in a spoke-and-wheel fashion, with the CEO at the center, allowing interactions across groups, but with the CEO in the loop on all activities.

Further breaking down the sales process into its functional parts, e.g., finding leads, closing the deal, and managing accounts, is another structural model that is typically reserved for a large organization. Each of these separate functions requires many employees, with their own structural needs and their own contributions to innovation. These contributions may be defined on a more granular level, such as participation on an internal innovation team or submitting a new idea.

Even within a large organization, the structure will determine how well these groups work together in the innovation culture. All too often the sales and marketing departments compete against each other rather than work in harmony. One of the major challenges of redesigning an organizational structure is to get these two bands playing the same song, in harmony, as they play their parts in the innovation program.

In smaller companies, other sales and marketing structures may be more helpful. Having fewer people means those people will be more likely to "wear more hats" and contribute to the entire sales process. They may cover marketing responsibilities, as well. While they may be strapped for time given these varied tasks, it is critical that they be part of the innovation effort for reasons already stated. They are the direct link to the customer, whose input is key to finding new opportunities. One of the best ways to accommodate this is with a customer database that is updated after each contact with the external customer. These databases are uniquely designed to reflect the product and/or services being sold and the collection of information related to their future needs.

Other non-traditional models can be used to trigger innovation, such as retaining a marketing research company or creativity consultant to help gather customer feedback and insights. Co-marketing collaborations with partners are a time-tested model for expanding the customer base and reaching out to new market areas that are ripe for innovation. These collaborations often stimulate innovation by bringing different perspectives of the challenges facing the marketplace and customer. To be successful, marketing collaborations require clear definition of content control and engagement expectations.

Larger sales structures often involve external and internal sales groups, with the external workforce responsible for the direct contact and finalization of sales, while the internal workforce offers support to the external salesforce as well as service to the customer following the sale. Both are in contact with customers and can capture their thoughts, comments, complaints, and suggestions for the innovation effort.

As sales models shift to be more technology driven and purchasing transactions are done online, the ratio of external sales to internal is changing in favor of internal. Outside sales reps spend increasing amounts of their time conducting remote sales activities, just like internal sales reps, and the differences between the two are fading (Figure 6.2,

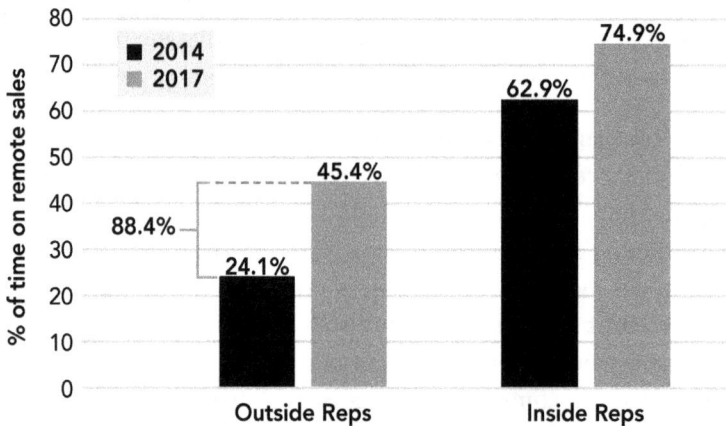

Figure 6.2   Time spent selling remotely.

(Adapted from Larsen 2020; used with permission.)

Time spent selling remotely; Larsen 2020). Internal sales models offer advantages in scalability, organizational growth due to reduced costs and increased access to customers, as well as the ability to access specific markets such as small businesses (Martin 2013). Organizational structures focused on internal sales groups may be challenged to have a complete view of the customer's situation, and companies with this model may need to ensure other means are in place to provide face-to-face access to customers.

SALES AND MARKETING ON THE INNOVATION TEAM

Marketing and sales have a double-barrel shotgun whose ammunition is innovation and whose target is acceptance by consumers/customers of the new product or service. The sales and marketing functions are deeply involved in the opportunity identification, creation, and delivery phase of the product cycle. Organizing the sales and marketing functions in a way that integrates them with the other functions of the innovation cycle is a must. They play a key role in capturing customer issues and pain points and are well positioned to develop open working relationships with customers, often in the customer's own environment. These relationships are critical for customers to feel comfortable sharing information and allowing themselves to be observed conducting their work processes, which is highly valuable for identifying innovation opportunities.

For the problem-solving phase of innovation, sales and marketing employees often have the network connections that are needed to approach customers with prototypes and early minimum viable products, seeking reactions and additional suggestions. They contribute key information regarding the value proposition for proposed solutions. The value proposition leads eventually to the concept for the marketing program, and having sales and marketing input at the early phases helps to ensure the reality of the marketplace is considered at every step of the innovation development.

As development continues, sales and marketing continue to be involved in obtaining user reactions to more refined versions of the innovation, coordinating delivery from and responses to the development team. In general, it is much harder for engineers to build these customer relationships and get this feedback themselves; sales and marketing employees are critical. The value proposition will likely evolve, too, and sales and marketing employees need to be part of those discussions.

Deploying the new solution relies heavily on the sales and marketing functions. Introducing new products, services, and business models results in an array of reactions. The early adopters will jump on the new concept, while the laggards will cling to the former model, even against a highly beneficial option. Sales and marketing are instrumental in helping customers along the range of adoption, based on those good relationships that were previously established. They are also positioned to enhance training programs and marketing materials to further roll out the innovation effectively and profitably.

Organizational structures in which sales and marketing are part of the innovation team at each step of the way help smooth transitions and leverage the synergies of cross-functional teams. People in sales and marketing tend to be practical people with good observation skills who can deliver and get the job done. Their involvement is most needed during development and deployment of the innovation, and their involvement, in terms of time and resource commitment, should be highest during these stages. That is not to say they aren't needed during the problem identification and solving phases — their involvement may be more limited in the early stages, but their perspective and ability to access customer pain points are important pieces of the upfront innovation process.

Every step of the sales and marketing cycle is an important candidate for innovation insight that directly impacts the value added to the consumer and/or the organization. The structure needs to leverage these contributions, enabling sales and marketing functions that can recognize potential opportunities; prepare realistic, accurate, and creative market specifications; and establish effective delivery models for the marketplace and users.

THE SUMMARY ON SALES AND MARKETING

Structuring your sales and marketing organizations for effective innovation means engaging them in all aspects of your innovation program. Sales and marketing employees are uniquely positioned to identify and understand your customers' pain points and problems, which are the key drivers of innovation. Setting expectations and supportive structures to capture those insights, and continuing to involve sales and marketing through innovation development to delivery to the marketplace are essential to a dynamic and innovative organization.

> *"Sales and marketing are the innovation heroes in most organizations."*

> – Dr. H. James Harrington

CHAPTER SEVEN

Structuring for Service Innovation

THE CUSTOMER EXPERIENCE

HAVE YOU EVER GOTTEN FRUSTRATED at the level of customer service you received? Did you give that organization a low online rating? Did you tell your friends and neighbors about it? It seems that bad news travels faster than good news, and in this day of online and instant reviews, many organizations have had to refocus their commitment to service to maintain customers and recruit new ones.

There is no doubt that having happy and enthused customers is worth the attention and focus you give them. Data show correlations between satisfaction measures and company growth/profitability. For example, Forrester conducts an annual customer experience index (CX). For the years 2010-2015, its data show compound average revenue growth of 17% for companies whose customers scored them highly (CX leaders), while CX laggards realized only 3% compound average revenue growth (Miller 2016). Best-in-class brands included USAA, several banks, Etsy, and Zappos, among others.

Customers are more likely to be satisfied — and organizations will experience all that comes with that satisfaction, namely, increased volumes of sales, recommendations to others, and retention and longevity — if their needs are met, but even more so if the organization makes the experience of being a customer simple and desirable. According to a recent XM Institute Insight Report (Temkin, Dorsey, and Segall 2019), customer experience ratings correlate directly with customer loyalty (see Table 7.1). The study included 10,000 U.S. consumers and their experiences across 294 companies in 20 industries.

Consumers who rated a company:	Very good	Poor
Were "very likely" to:		
Make further purchases	94%	49%
Give positive recommendations	95%	47%
Trust the company	90%	40%
Forgive a bad experience	75%	39%
Try out new products	64%	28%

Table 7.1   Correlation of consumer experience ratings with customer loyalty measures.   (Temkin, Dorsey, and Segall 2019)

There is no single point of interaction that determines customer satisfaction, but rather, it's the entire experience, over time and with multiple interactions. Structuring your organization for innovation in service delivery requires a broad approach that covers the entire customer experience, and it can pay off handsomely in customer loyalty and business volume. How can you organize your business to avoid poor customer reactions, innovate your service offerings, and get your customers excited about your services? Structural models that can help you do this are further described in this chapter.

FOCUS ON THE CUSTOMER

A key factor in service innovation is making sure your organization's structure puts the customer first. Yes, you may think you do this, but ask yourself the following questions:

- When customers interact with your organization, do they interact with a machine or a human? What is required for customers to reach a human if they need to? Is that process efficient or cumbersome?

- Do you know how your customers feel about your processes for customer access? Are multiple options available, e.g., in person, website, social media, etc.? Can they easily choose the type of contact they prefer?

- How are your back-office operations employees connected to your customers? Are there multiple layers between them? Are your product developers talking to customers, or to sales and marketing staff or others who are interpreting and translating the customers' positions and needs?

- Do your employees who are in direct contact with customers understand their responsibilities related to human interactions? Do they possess adequate people skills such as empathy and compassion? Does your structure ensure they are trained in these skills?

- Is your physical layout conducive to idea sharing, collaboration, and workforce interactions? Do your employees enjoy downtime in which to share customer feedback and new ideas and elaborate on them? See Appendix B, Open Office, for more information.

- Are service issues dealt with quickly and effectively? Has the individual who is in direct contact with the customer been given the authority to grant the customer additional benefits without first checking with the management team? A customer's satisfaction level goes down by 40% per each person they have to talk to before they are satisfied with the way the situation is being handled.

These are some of the important components of a service organization structured for innovation. Let's explore them in more detail.

It's easy in the day-to-day efforts of running a business to become inwardly focused, making sure production is on track, financial matters are being managed, problems and issues are being addressed, and personnel are getting the work done and being paid. Strategies are developed, perhaps focusing on new products or market areas, and managers are keeping everything moving. Customers are part of that mix, of course, but sometimes they may get subordinated to all the other activities going on, and this is where things may go awry for the organization. Keeping the customer front and center, and tying everyone's perspective back to the customer, is paramount.

Crafting your operational processes from the customer's view is a good way to ensure this customer focus. It can be done by changing the way you map your processes. Traditionally, work processes are mapped from the employee's perspective, spelling out individual roles and responsibilities, procedural steps, handoffs, and necessary resources to conduct the process. The focus is on making sure all employees know their required steps and how to do them, where their work connects with other processes and departments, and how efficiency is driven through process standardization. In fact, customers may be left out of the process design because the organization has little control over them or their contribution to the process.

To shift the focus to be more customer-centric, rethink your procedures from a customer experience perspective. One way to do this is to build a service blueprint, a method that describes the organization's key processes from the customer service point of view (see Appendix B, Service Blueprinting). Start by listing all the possible points of contact customers have with the organization. Consider all the ways in which the organization has visibility into the customer; these are the stages on which your customer sees you perform (see Figure 7.1). These touch-points might include telephone, email, and social media contacts, as well

Figure 7.1 Performing for the customer.

as face-to-face meetings by appointment or more casually at professional conferences and meetings, or other written correspondence. Each of these types of contacts may reach your organization in different ways, e.g., contact with an employee, automated call system, or third-party answering service. Map each of these processes from the customer to the internal on-stage employee or system responsible for receiving and handling the contact.

Start with the face-to-face options, then move on to mapping the indirect contact methods (e.g., emails, phone calls). Think about how each process is perceived by the customer, how efficiently (from the customer's view) it works, and how well the customer's requests are addressed in each process. Continue to map your processes from the individual or system receiving the customer inquiry to the steps for responding to them—those steps that are backstage and "behind the curtain" to the customer. How are the responses customized? How easy is it for the customer to get additional information if the first response is not satisfactory? How are responses tracked for follow-up? As you drill down into the organization's processes, you should eventually get to product development and delivery work areas, and ultimately to the infrastructure processes such as accounting and financing and facilities management.

Viewing the work of the organization in this way allows you to make innovative changes to the structure of your organization and focus it on the customer experience (see Figure 7.2). It also emphasizes to every employee how their work supports customers and the business. This approach can be transformative, moving beyond incremental improvements of existing processes and exposing opportunities to innovate the entire customer service model. Only when you see things form the customers' eyes can you add value and develop enthusiastic customers (Bitner, Ostrom, and Morgan 2008; Bollard et al. 2017).

Similar to service blueprinting, customer journey mapping is based on the sequence or phases of the customer's experiences with the organization. This approach looks at the steps and interactions the customer goes through to find the organization, understand your product/service offerings, make a purchase, and follow up with questions or complaints. Diagramming this series of events is called customer journey mapping,

The Anatomy of a Service Blueprint

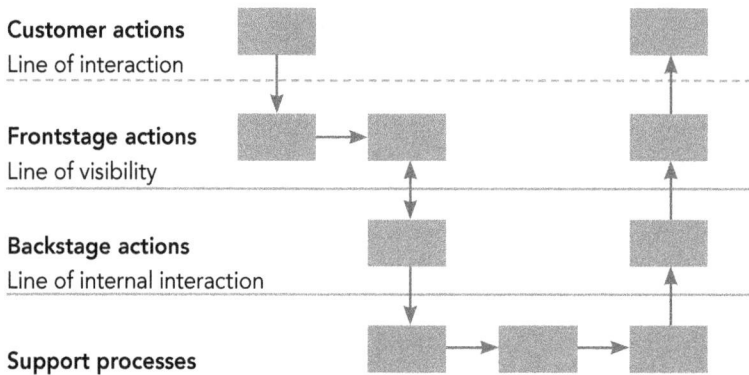

Customer actions
Line of interaction

Frontstage actions
Line of visibility

Backstage actions
Line of internal interaction

Support processes

Figure 7.2 Service blueprint model.   (Adapted from Cram 2015)

and it is a useful way to understand the challenges facing customers and potential customers when working with the organization. For example, the journey map may start with early advertising and marketing campaigns, and proceed through initial customer contact and purchase decision steps, delivery of the product or service, and long-term loyalty building. The customer journey map is a visualization of the series of customer interactions with the organization that delves deeply into the details of those experiences (see Figure 7.3). It is used to identify where customer perceptions differ from what the organization's employees think the customer perceives. The risks associated with poor customer experiences can be assessed, with resulting identification of opportunities for enhancing the customer's experience. Studies show that a positive customer experience is the critical factor, over product quality and cost, in securing a customer's satisfaction and business (Weir 2018).

Now that you have a better understanding of the organization's workflow relative to the customer experience, it is a good idea to recognize that customers value simplicity. No one likes to go through multiple hoops to get to the service or information they need. Being shunted from one service department to another, from email to website, or from online chatroom to phone call, is frustrating and inefficient. What's more, no one wants to be in a queue waiting, even if the wait time has been stated upfront.

User experience

Life-cycle stage	Visit website	Register	Onboard	Convert & retain
Touch points & scorecard	• Site design • Messaging • Content	• Call-to-action button • Registration form	• Tool tips • Serf-serve • Integrations • Documentation	• Nuture emails • Payment process • Calls-to-action • Pricing & offers
Challenges	• Undifferentiated messaging • Small content supply	• Untested CTAs • Awkward registration form design	• Lack tool tips • Onboarding not yet intuitive • Thin documentation	• Only have system emails • Untested offers and pricing

Recommendation

	Visit website	Register	Onboard	Convert & retain
Metrics	• Bounce rate • Conversion % • CTA button click %	• Registration % by channel	• % who integrate Mixpanel • % who create scenario • % who invite others	• User-to-paid conversion % • Churn % • Customer LTV
Improvement opportunities	1. AB test messaging 2. Home page video 3. Customer testimonials	1. AB test CTA button 2. Test registration form (if possible)	1. Rollout tool tips 2. Research onboarding with live testers 3. Continue support material rollout	1. Link blog content to nurture flows 2. Test offers to inform pricing

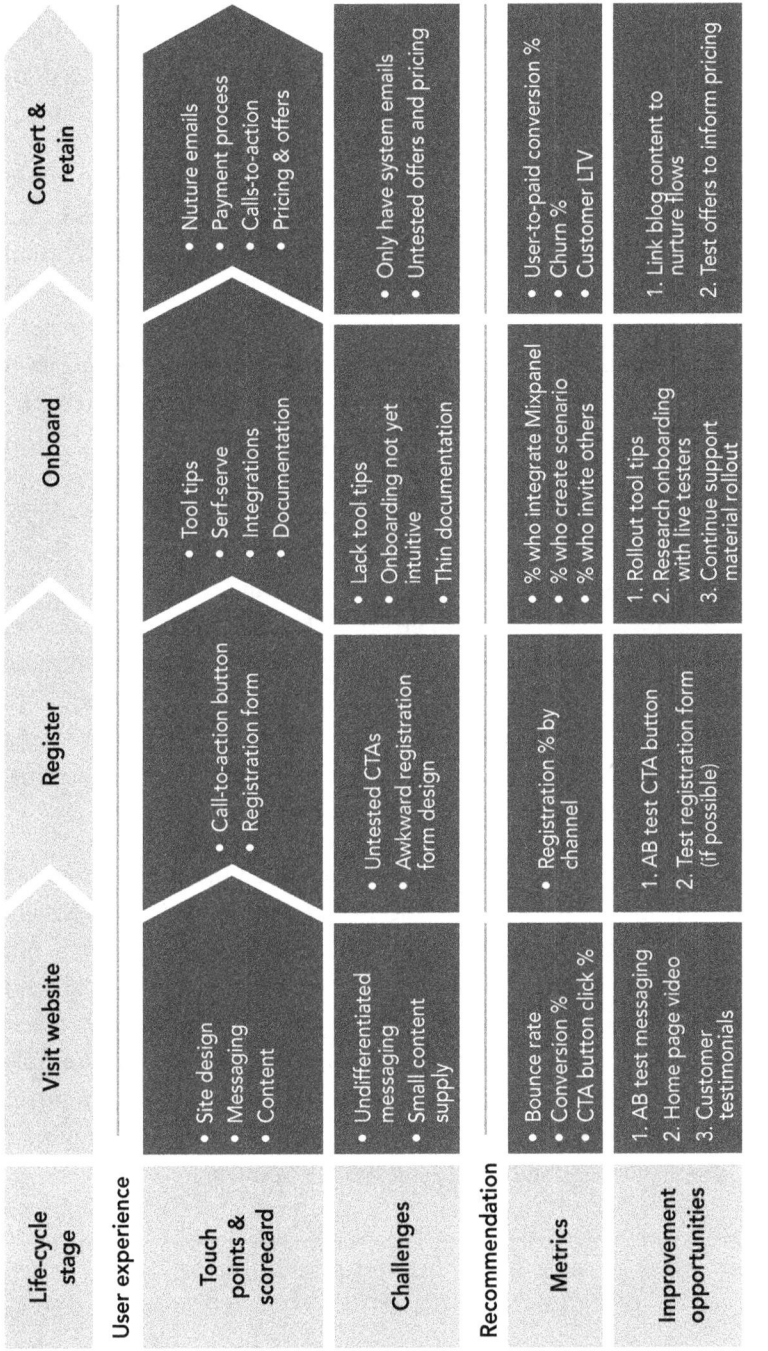

(Adapted from Gaid 2019)

Figure 7.3 Customer journey map model.

Structuring your service organization to minimize these detractions will help build loyal and happy customers, and using technology is a key element to achieve this, especially for larger organizations (see Chapter 5, Technology).

Electronic customer relationship management systems (eCRM) provide the technology that allows customers to engage virtually with the organization to submit orders and queries and to obtain information about their account and the company's products. These systems must be easy for the customer to use and should make it simple for them to reach out for additional information when needed. Benefits to the organization are the ability to log and track customer interactions, quickly access the information that is needed to address the customer request, and build customer history data to help provide continuity and consistency in interactions over time. eCRMs may provide automated answering scripts and workflows, with customer self-serve options and standard response information, building in features and efficiencies for the customer and for the organization as well. They can be set up to trigger follow-up actions so the organization can proactively reach out to customers at key time points in the customer life cycle, such as release of a new product version. Data from the eCRM can and should be reviewed and analyzed by the organization to establish customer trends, quality of service interactions, and opportunities to innovate the customer experience.

Use of technology for the delivery of services must not detract from the customer experience and is not a replacement for promptly and effectively responding to the customer. It is important that the electronic process not be simply a digitization of existing cumbersome procedures; it should be as efficient and streamlined as possible, both for the customer and the organization. Long wait times, impersonal interactions, and multiple transfers will quickly discourage customers and drive them elsewhere for a better experience. Adding efficiency is one way the eCRM can innovate your service model and add value for your customers.

UNDERSTAND THE EMPLOYEE-CUSTOMER RELATIONSHIP

Building an organizational structure that drives innovation in services relies heavily on the humans involved. Service industries are based on personal interactions between customers and employees—often face-to-face meetings or voice-to-voice conversations—and these interactions are the crux of customer satisfaction. This is where value is added to the service delivery.

> *You can't measure and manage the employee and customer experience as separate entities. Because you must manage these human systems in tandem, you may need to reorganize.*
>
> – J. H. Fleming and Jim Asplund
> (Fleming and Asplund 2007).

Given the critical-to-success nature of the customer-employee relationship, it is best to manage them together, not separately. Consider organizational structures that put employee management (i.e., HR) together with customer relationship management (operations, quality, or marketing); this emphasizes the critical relationship between the two and their importance for organization success. You must identify internally who owns this relationship and ensure it is managed as an integrated system. Acknowledge that each customer/employee interaction is unique and develop processes to allow customized services for each service interaction. Define innovation skills as part of employees' responsibilities, and provide the necessary support to develop those skills (Appendix B, Skills).

Monitoring employee and customer relationships is as important, if not more important, to assessing organizational health than financial measures because they are leading indicators, while financial metrics are always lagging. However, because they are dependent on human nature, service interactions are not easily measured or standardized in the way that, say, automated processes are.

Emotion frames the employee-customer encounter.
It is important not to think like an economist or
an engineer when you're assessing employee-
customer interactions. Emotions, it turns out,
inform both sides' judgements and behavior even
more powerfully than rational or dispassionate
thinking. Because employees and customers are
people first and employees or customers second,
they are prone to all the volatility and irrationality
that is the hallmark of being human.

– J. H. Fleming and Jim Asplund, 2007

Make sure your structures consider the emotional side of service. As the old saying goes, "Perception is reality," and these are not objective experiences. Of the elements of the customer experience—emotion, success, and effort—customers are more likely to demonstrate loyalty behaviors, such as repeat purchases and recommendations, if their customer experience was satisfying from an emotional perspective than if their experience was successful or easy to complete (see Table 7.2).

	Emotion[1]	Success[1]	Effort[1]
Likelihood to:			
Purchase more	91%	84%	85%
Recommend company	93%	84%	86%

[1] *High customer experience rating*

Table 7.2 The role of customer emotion in experience perceptions.
(Adapted from Temkin, Dorsey, and Segall 2019)

We know customers are satisfied on two levels: rationally and emotionally. *Emotionally* satisfied customers are more likely to tell other people, buy more often and in greater volumes, and stay with the organization longer. Perhaps surprisingly, *rationally* satisfied customers exhibit the same behaviors as dissatisfied customers; they are less likely to be loyal customers and more likely to shop around for other service providers even though technically they say they are satisfied.

Much has been learned in the past 20 years about how humans make decisions and react to situations, and it is often illogical and unpredictable. It turns out that emotions contribute more to decision-making than rational thought. Our rational, well-thought-out responses and decisions are often overruled by our intuitive and quick thinking, which may or may not be to our best advantage. This intuitive quick thinking is subject to the context in which decisions are framed, as shown by Amos Tversky and Daniel Kahneman (Kahneman 2013). In their study, individuals were asked to make two decisions after considering the options for both decisions:

Decision 1: Choose between (A) a sure gain of $240 or (B) a 25% chance to gain $1,000 and a 75% chance to gain nothing.

Decision 2: Choose between (C) a sure loss of $750 or (D) a 75% chance to lose $1,000 and a 25% chance to lose nothing.

The majority of respondents chose (A) and (D). Their initial (i.e., emotional) reaction went with the sure thing — gaining money in Decision 1 and not losing money in Decision 2. Had they calculated the comparative results of the four possible combinations of answers, however, they would most likely have rationally chosen (B) and (C), which can also be stated as a 25% chance to win $250 and a 75% chance to lose $750 dollars, instead of (A) and (D), which results in a 25% chance to win $240 and a 75% chance to lose $760 (Kahneman 2013). When the researchers conducted this experiment, only 3% of respondents chose the B/C combination, while 73% chose the A/D combination, illustrating how strong the emotional, gut reaction drives our decision-making.

Understanding how humans make decisions is an important element of innovative service delivery and innovation in general. In fact, psychological studies of human reactions, biases, and heuristics in judgements have spawned the field of behavioral economics — the application of the science behind how we think to our economic decision-making. Alain Samson described behavioral economics as the field of study "which suggests that human decisions are strongly influenced by context, including the way in which choices are presented to us. Behavior varies across time and space, and it is subject to cognitive biases, emotions, and social influences. Decisions are the result of less deliberative, linear, and controlled processes than we would like to believe" (Samson 2014).

Tools and processes can be used to help make the service transaction more efficient, but these will not be sufficient to achieve the highest service performance or financial benefit. Use available tools to help get at and understand customers' service needs and opportunities, such as QFD, net promoter score, and Kano (see Appendix B).

For employees, creating a structure that drives service innovation includes being clear about the expectations for innovative thinking. To ensure a workforce with the necessary skills, you must first identify the traits that improve success in service delivery. To organize for innovation, you need to build a workforce that understands it and has the skills that are needed to be innovative. Successful innovation requires both managers and employees. Service employees are typically your front lines for communicating with customers, and they are sources of many innovative ideas. These critical contributions must be supported by management by establishing clear priorities and committing necessary resources.

Develop hiring methods that identify and bring innovative thinkers into the organization. Job descriptions should include responsibilities for problem-solving and capturing customer concerns and wishes, as well as influencing customers to adopt new and innovative offerings. Required expertise needs to include creativity and intersocial skills. Provide training in innovation concepts and tools and develop career advancement opportunities in innovation management. And, don't forget to reinforce innovative behaviors by recognizing and rewarding those service interactions that result in delighted customers.

> *"We hire passionate people, and we balance cold realism with business passion."*
>
> – Wendell Weeks, CEO, Corning

Look to your quality professionals, who already possess many of the innovation skills and expertise you will need. In addition to supporting your innovation organization, they can become teachers and mentors to others in your workforce. For example, creativity and problem-solving are key competencies in addressing today's business challenges and opportunities; quality managers and engineers are skilled in a variety of creative problem-solving tools.

Furthermore, interactions and collaborations with customers are important sources of innovative ideas and customer delight. Ensuring customers have opportunities to convey and discuss their thoughts, for example, through instant pop-up surveys, focus groups, and prototype reviews, helps to build open relationships and gather the diverse perspectives of your customers. These interactions with customers may enhance the structure for innovation by extending them beyond the service provider to other internal groups, such as product developers, marketing, process improvement experts, and executive management.

LINK THE FRONT END OF SERVICE INNOVATION TO THE OPERATIONAL SIDE

All of this points to the development of a strong service management system in your organization, that is, "an all-encompassing management system meant to bring together all aspects of organization management such as: Planning, Strategies, Policies, Objectives, Documentation, and Processes…into a service-oriented organization," as defined by techopedia.com (2020). Only by establishing an overarching system can you be assured that the front line of your service organization is adequately linked to operations (see Chapter 2, Front-Back Structure). This linkage is necessary to successfully carry out the innovation cycle of opportunity identification through problem-solving, development, and execution. This is the exciting work that results in customer delight and organizational success!

Service Innovation Metrics

Within this service management system, you can identify touchpoints between individuals and units, build in efficiencies, and create a structure that is tuned for regular changes, including major innovations as well as more incremental improvements. You will be able to pinpoint key metrics to provide data for solid decision-making and create effective tools to gather that information (e.g., design of surveys). Ensuring the selection of metrics that align with desired performance outcomes is essential to getting the most out of the data but is often overlooked as the metrics are established. Collecting data that sit in a report and are not actionable is a waste of resources that no organization can afford.

So how can you objectively monitor and manage these subjective service activities? Organizations commonly use satisfaction surveys of customers and employees, and these can be valuable if the right questions are asked and the data are analyzed objectively. Be sure to include metrics for service integration between employee and customer. Metrics for customer satisfaction are similar to those for employee satisfaction, and both are relevant to assess the adequacy of service delivery. Selecting the survey tool that is best suited to the audience, designing questions to elicit the information you need (i.e., actionable), and capturing results using appropriate scales or free text are all factors in conducting effective surveys for customer or employee feedback. The data to be collected and the analyses to be conducted must be preplanned to obtain objective feedback. See Chapter 4, Understanding Customer Needs and How to Add Value, for additional information on surveys.

One simple tool, the net promoter score (NPS), provides insights into the overall customer position regarding the organization (i.e., promoters, passives, and detractors; see Appendix B, Net Promoter Score). Overall NPS results will likely need to be analyzed in more detail to tease out specific issues, ideas, and individual situations and help make sense of the information. The effort is worth it when you can leverage the inputs of customers who are happy and engaged with your services and turn them into incentives for new customers (Hyken 2016).

As with any metric, NPS will only be helpful if the information is used to drive innovation and value-adding changes, and it should be part of a set of metrics used to assess service delivery and customer satisfaction. Other service innovation metrics include customer retention/attrition, and sales figures by customer, volume and/or dollar value, and percent market share. Making sure you are asking the right questions in the right way, and then objectively analyzing that information, is key.

THE BOTTOM LINE

The key to structuring your organization for innovative services is to focus on the customer experience. Develop processes that are driven from the customer's point of view and aligned through to back-end work that is not directly facing the customer. Employees are integral to the customer relationship, and providing them with good training, tools, and expectations for innovation is a must. Tracking the customer experience with actionable metrics, and acting on the results to add new services that delight them, is the bottom line.

CHAPTER EIGHT

Structuring for Innovation: Should You Reorganize?

MANY ORGANIZATIONS TODAY ARE looking for ways to be more innovative. Competition is fierce, and the pressure to find the next big disruptor is intense. Careers are made or broken on the success of innovative endeavors. Should you reorganize to improve your chances of successful innovation?

A structural reorganization may be just the thing you need. As we've shown in this book, the organization's structure can be a significant enhancer of innovation by supporting a culture of creativity and agility, clarifying expectations around the organization's innovative path forward, and encouraging the adaptability that is needed in a highly innovative organization.

Traditional hierarchical models are often too bureaucratic, cumbersome, and slow, inhibiting rather than supporting innovation. Relying on top leaders for new ideas can lead to failure to recognize opportunities early or a lack of outside-the-box thinking. Waiting for necessary approvals at each step of the hierarchy not only slows down the process but the passion and fervor of the innovators may also start to wane as they wait for permission to move forward. Meanwhile, the competition has more time to develop their offerings and get them before yours.

More and more, organizations are looking at network models of organization. Loosening the structure to allow more interactions, information exchange, and collaborations among employees, customers, and partners/suppliers triggers new ideas, increases the speed of development, and generally improves the rate and success of innovation. Network structures are more likely to provide the diverse inputs that lead to new and creative solutions, as well as the agility that is needed to move quickly to a market-ready offering. This speed is essential in the fast-paced age of instant communication, global communities, and increasing competition from all sides.

In fact, today's technologies are useful tools that help implement and manage the networked organization. Online communications, including social media, electronic messenger applications and email, as well as electronic tools such as project trackers and strategy maps, allow distant team members to work together easily. Readily searchable information, available in an instant, allows more rapid insights into problems and the development of solutions. New technologies turn up every day; monitoring these technological advancements allows rapid assessment and identification of those technologies you might be able to adopt for your own innovative offering. Harnessing the advantages of technology to drive your structure is an important part of innovation.

If you think your organization could be more innovative by adopting a less hierarchical, more networked structure, then a reorganization may be what you need. Be careful not to reorganize for the sake of reorganizing, however. Reorganizations are disruptive, put people on edge, and can backfire if not done carefully. Up to 80% of reorganizations do not deliver on the expected value, and 10% cause real damage to the company (Orgchart 2019).

Be sure you understand what your objectives are and how you think a new structure can help achieve them. In their book, *ReOrg: How to Get it Right,* Stephen Heidari-Robinson and Suzanne Heywood (Heidari-Robinson and Heywood 2016), describe five reorganization steps that can improve business results and shorten the time to implementation. These steps are: (1) set the business goals of the reorganization; (2) take time to diagnose what's right and what's wrong with your current organization before moving forward; (3) design an organization that covers structure, people, and process; (4) plan the implementation properly; and (5) check that the new organization delivers what it is supposed to deliver.

It may be helpful to have each member of the executive team sign off on a document that numerically defines the advantages and disadvantages the reorganization will have on the parts of the organization that report to him or her. Signing these documents cements an agreement between the individual and the organization that becomes part of the individual's salary and bonus plan.

Determining the business goals and objectives for the reorganization will benefit from the involvement of others, both internal and external to the organization. The exercise of coming up with the objectives forces a thorough and deep review of the organization's purpose and desired directions. Once these are clear, the organizational structure can be set up to ensure they are effectively pursued. The head of engineering at Instagram, James Everingham, with his leadership team, developed a list of 20 desired outcomes from their planned reorganization and ranked them by priority (Everingham 2017). The top five became their organizational principles:

- "Minimize dependencies between teams and code"

- "Have clear accountability with the fewest decision makers"

- "Groups have clear measures"

- "Top-level organizations have roadmaps"

- "Performance, stability, and code quality have owners"

The new structure was built around these principles. For example, a core infrastructure team was established to bring together teams that formerly had duplicative responsibilities. Other teams were created based on key priorities; each team had a clear focus area, such as engagement or business platform. Roles and accountabilities within these groups were clearly defined, leading to improved employee satisfaction. The new structure was less complex, more readily scalable, and supported faster execution than the former model, even as the number of engineers quadrupled. By determining their objectives first, the company was able to design a customized structure that worked for it.

RESTRUCTURING CONSIDERATIONS BASED ON INNOVATION IMPROVEMENT AREA

You may choose to focus your reorganization efforts on one or more of the five areas in which innovation improvement thrives. The information you collect from internal and external sources will help you determine in which areas your efforts will be most productive.

Restructuring for Management Innovation

If management presents obstacles to innovation and prevents the organization from excelling, your restructuring efforts need to (see Chapter 3):

- Emphasize the customer and the customer experience

- Build an internal environment that is more agile and comfortable with failure

- Provide sufficient resources at the right time in the innovation cycle

- Serve as a catalyst for innovation

There are many models that may work for you, but blindly adopting one of them will likely be less effective than determining your goals and your current state, than creating your own model that addresses the gaps and meets your desired state.

Management must also build a structure that is attractive to the various types of people who are needed to innovate. The structure must give them the space to create, collaborate, and succeed, enhancing the organization's performance as well as their own.

Restructuring for Product Innovation

If your products or other offerings are your biggest challenge in innovation, your restructuring efforts need to (see Chapter 4):

- Identify responsibilities for understanding customer behaviors and pain points

- Develop expertise in methods and tools to understand customer thinking

- Establish flexible change management methods for product development and life-cycle management

- Support your innovation pipeline and risk-based portfolio

Aligning the organization's core competencies, resources, and strategic direction with the customer's processes, frustrations, and inefficiencies is the sweet spot where your organization can address the customer's issues innovatively. Build your structure to ensure this alignment and your product innovation will benefit.

Restructuring for Process Innovation

If your processes are stuck in an endless cycle of minor tweaks for efficiencies and cost reduction, with no thought for innovation, or if you don't have an innovation process, your restructuring efforts will need to change that. Historically, innovation has been addressed through R&D departments or product marketing groups. Newer structural models are being implemented that broaden the responsibilities for innovation and integrate them into other parts of the organization, such as operations. These models bring about more of the collaboration, idea and information exchange, and rapid communications so important to innovation. The structure may include innovation coaching and mentoring groups to help anchor the innovation process and deploy it company-wide.

Your innovation process needs to set expectations for the responsibilities and activities associated with innovation. The process needs to succeed in an environment of uncertainty; it must be highly iterative and non-linear, and you should be able to enter and exit it at any point. Those responsible for the process need to understand there will be many loops back to earlier points in the process as more is learned about the problem and its innovative solution. This is normal, expected, and necessary!

A common innovation methodology supports efficient communications and activities, reduces wasted time and misuse of resources, and keeps those responsible pointed in the right strategic direction. All innovation processes include steps related to identifying the problem/opportunity, coming up with creative solutions and validating them, fine-tuning the best solution and enhancing its value, and deploying the solution to the users and customers who will realize the value (and pay for it). Many of the core concepts of quality management are useful for the innovation process, as well, such as plan-do-check-act (PDCA), decision and prioritization tools, and risk assessment methodologies.

Supporting processes may include procedures for collecting and analyzing market and customer data, value analysis, decision-making, risk management, and change management. Organizational structures that include parallel processing, colocation, and automation are often found to be useful in the innovation process.

Building a structure that drives your innovation process is a core element of the successful innovative organization (see Chapter 5).

Restructuring for Sales and Marketing Innovation

If your sales and marketing groups have become isolated from the rest of the company or have been slow to contribute to identifying new opportunities, your restructuring effort will need to emphasize the responsibilities of sales and marketing to talk to and understand the customer (see Chapter 6). As the primary interface with the customer in many organizations, sales and marketing staff must bring their insights and observations into the organization's innovation effort. They are also pivotal in deploying new offerings and helping the customer understand the value provided for them.

Sales and marketing organizational structures that are not hierarchical but rather fluid and constantly shifting tend to be the most innovative, allowing access to customers and internal employees as needed, without going through layers of structure to get the necessary information. The structure also needs to avoid groups within sales and marketing from competing against each other. If you are using or moving toward a more automated sales model, as many organizations are, your structure may shift to a greater focus on your internal sales team and how your customers react to the automation.

Sales and marketing staff are critical members of the innovation team, playing a role at each step of the way. Besides bringing customer feedback and insights forward, they often have the network connections that are needed to gather user inputs through prototypes and early minimum viable products. They can also play a role in improving the value of the solution in the optimization phase, and they are critical in the deployment of a new offering. Your restructuring needs to engage sales and marketing in all aspects of your innovation program.

Restructuring for Service Innovation

If your services are subpar, with poor customer engagement scores, too many customer complaints, and low customer retention, your restructuring may be able to help if you organize from the customer's point of view (see Chapter 7). Ask yourself how the "customer sees it" for every potential customer interaction, and link that back to the supporting structures that are not directly part of the customer interaction. This exercise can be highly revealing and can expose complacency within your organization regarding the customer focus.

Again, automation is likely to be a part of the service structure, with eCRMs taking on many transactions that were previously done in person or on the phone. Many customers prefer this because of the efficiencies for them, but make sure that is true for your customers. Even the best system will have trouble with some challenging customer interactions; your structure needs to account for these situations as well as the normal, run-of-the-mill interactions.

Organizing for service involves not only the customer but also the employee with whom the customer interacts. The customer-employee interaction is perhaps the most important relationship in your organization, and combining the organizational structure for employee management and customer relationship management makes sense for many organizations. This can be challenging because of the emotional element in these groups; understanding personality types and customer decision-making behaviors may be key skill sets within your structure.

STRUCTURING FOR INNOVATION

There are many structure models to choose from (see Chapter 2), or better yet, design your own! One of them, or perhaps a combination of types, will be the best answer for your situation. The challenge is to find the right structure and fit for your organization, and then deploy it. Our intent in this book is to trigger the reader's creative mind to begin thinking about structural changes that can lead to greater innovation, successful offerings, and satisfied stakeholders.

Start by looking at the organization from three perspectives: strategic, operational, and tactical (see Chapter 1):

- The strategic perspective looks at the organization from the top down and determines the overall shape of the organization. It is a process of moving the big boxes around to determine the right fit. This is where management innovation is incredibly important.

- The operational perspective deals with strategic business units. Review the strategic fit by looking from the top down. Review the appropriate mix of operational, managerial, and support processes through a bottom-up review. Product, service, and sales and marketing are key areas of operational innovation.

- The tactical perspective is completed with a bottom-up approach and determines the work team and job designs. Process innovation plays a key role here.

It is the combination of strategic, operational, and tactical decisions that will be the basis for determining the right organizational structure and, if done well, can drive a structure that is highly successful at innovation.

APPENDIX A

References and Citations

Abernathy, W. J., and J. M. Utterback. 1978. "Patterns of Innovation in Technology." *Technology Review* 80, no. 7.

Agius, Aaron. 2020. How to Create an Effective Customer Journey Map. Accessed June 3, 2020. https://blog.hubspot.com/service/customer-journey-map.

Alsever, Jennifer. 2015. "Startups… inside giant companies." https://fortune.com/2015/04/26/startups-inside-giant-companies/.

Alspach, Kyle. 2019. "CRN Exclusive: HP to Launch New Organizational Structure, Appoint First-Ever Chief Commercial Officer." https://www.crn.com/news/channel-programs/crn-exclusive-hp-to-launch-new-organizational-structure-appoint-first-ever-chief-commercial-officer#:~:text=and%20Technology%20Integrators-,CRN%20Exclusive%3A%20HP%20To%20Launch%20New%20Organizational%20Structure%2C%20Appoint%20First,president%20of%20its%20print%20business.

Alter, Adam. 2013. "How to Build a Collaborative Office Space Like Pixar and Google." https://99u.adobe.com/articles/16408/how-to-build-a-collaborative-office-space-like-pixar-and-google.

Amazon. 2020. "Amazon AWS Big Data Tools Website." Amazon. Accessed February 13, 2020. https://aws.amazon.com/getting-started/use-cases/big-data/.

Anderson, Ken. 2009. "Ethnographic Research: A Key to Strategy." *Harvard Business Review* (March).

ASQ. n.d. The Corning Journey to Perform Excellence: Innovation Spanning Three Centuries. https://asq.org/quality-resources/case-studies-corning

Bersin, Joshua. 2016. "The New Organization: Different by Design." Accessed May 1, 2016. http://joshbersin.com/2016/03/THE-NEW-ORGANIZATION-DIFFERENT-BY-DESIGN/.

Bhalla, A. 2010. Celebrating the Demise of Quality — Long Live Innovation, *Quality Digest.*

Bitner M. J., A. L. Ostrom, and F. N. Morgan. 2008. "Service Blueprinting: A Practical Technique for Service Innovation." *California Management Review* 50, no. 3:66-94.

Bollard, Albert, Elixabete Larrea, Alex Singla, and Rohit Sood. 2017. "The Next-Generation Operating Model for the Digital World." https://www.mckinsey.com/business-functions/mckinsey-digital/our-insights/the-next-generation-operating-model-for-the-digital-world#.

Box, George E. P., and William H. Woodall. 2012. "Innovation, Quality Engineering, and Statistics." *Quality Engineering* 24, no. 1:20-29.

Buckman, Jim, and Mary Beth Buckman. 2013. "Reinventing Excellence." *Quality Progress* 46, no. 7:34-40.

Burkus, David. 2016. *Under New Management: How Leading Organizations Are Upending Business as Usual.* Boston: Houghton Mifflin Harcourt.

Christensen, Clayton M. 1997. *The Innovator's Dilemma: When New Technologies Cause Great Firms to Fail. The Management of Innovation and Change Series.* Boston: Harvard Business School Press.

Cram, J. 2015. The Marketing Technology Myth; MarTech, San Francisco https://www.slideshare.net/MarTechConf/the-marketing-technology-myth-connecting-systems-and-experiences/26

Creasey, Timothy J., Robert Stise, Alex FitzSimons, Alana Birky, and Prosci (Firme). 2016. *Best Practices in Change Management 2016: 1120 Participants Share Lessons and Best Practices in Change Management,* 9th edition. Loveland, CO: Prosci. texte.

Davenport, Thomas H., and Nitin Nohria. 1994. "Case Management and the Integration of Labor." *MIT Sloan Management Review* (Winter).

Day, Ryan. 2020. "IIoT, Coronavirus, and the Supply Chain." Accessed June 3, 2020. https://www.qualitydigest.com/inside/innovation-column/iiot-coronavirus-and-supply-chain-051920.html?utm_source=MadMimi&utm_medium=email&utm_content=IIoT+and+the +supply+chain+++Lean+and+agile%3A+the+catch&utm_campaign=20200601_m158632446_QD+6-02-20+Hitachi&utm_term=IIoT_2C+Coronavirus_ 2C+and+the+Supply+Chain_0D_0A_0D _0A_0D_0A.

Deloitte. 2016. Global Human Capital Trends 2016. "The New Organizations: Different by Design." Bersin, Geller, Wakefield and Walsh. https://www2.deloitte.com/us/en/insights/focus/human-capital-trends/2016/human-capital-trends-introduction.html

DiBenedetto, Alexa, Roger Hoerl, and Ronald D. Snee. 2014. "Solving Jigsaw Puzzles." *Quality Progress* 47, no. 6:50-53.

Dudovskiy, John. 2018. "Amazon Organizational Structure." https://research-methodology.net/amazon-organizational-structure-2/.

Dyer, Jeffrey H., Hal B. Gregersen, and Clayton Christensen 2009. "The Innovator's DNA." *Harvard Business Review* (December).

Eriksson, Martin. 2017. "Innovation is Broken by Janice Fraser." (August 25). https://www.mindtheproduct.com/innovation-broken-janice-fraser/.

Everingham, James. 2017. "How We Reorganized Instagram's Engineering Team While Quadrupling Its Size." *Harvard Business Review.*

Fairchild, Greg, and Gerry Yemen. 2014. "Case in Point: Casket Business Triumphs, Diversifies through Acquisitions." *Washington Post.* Accessed Feb. 27, 2020. https://www.washingtonpost.com/business/case-in-point-casket-business-triumphs-diversifies-through-acquisitions/2014/01/10/ebcdcdb6-762f-11e3-b1c5-739e63e9c9a7_story.html.

Fleming, John Howland, and Jim Asplund. 2007. *Human Sigma: Managing the Employee-Customer Encounter.* New York: Gallup Press.

Forbes Insights. 2014. "Culture of Quality: Accelerating Growth and Performance in the Enterprise." Forbes.com.

Fowler, Bree. 2019. "Best Cell-Phone Companies: Is Bigger Better?" https://www.consumerreports.org/cell-phone-service-providers/best-cell-phone-companies-is-bigger-better/.

Furr, Nathan R., and Jeff Dyer. 2014. *The Innovator's Method: Bringing the Lean Startup into Your Organization.* Boston: Harvard Business Review Press.

Gaid, A. 2019. Everything You Need to Know about Making a Customer Journey Map; https://www.oberlo.com/blog/customer-journey-map

Greenwald, Ted. 2012. "Business Model Canvas: A Simple Tool For Designing Innovative Business Models." https://www.forbes.com/sites/tedgreenwald/2012/01/31/business-model-canvas-a-simple-tool-for-designing-innovative-business-models/#4432e1f916a7.

Griswold, Alison, and Jason Karaian. 2018. "It Took Amazon 14 Years to Make as Much in Net Profit as It Did Last Quarter." https://qz.com/1196256/it-took-amazon-amzn-14-years-to-make-as-much-net-profit-as-it-did-in-the-fourth-quarter-of-2017/.

Halzack, Sarah. 2017. "Under Armour debuts 'made in the U.S.' gear — and tests what we think we know about manufacturing in America." *Washington Post.* (January 30). Accessed February 14, 2020. https://www.washingtonpost.com/news/business/wp/2017/01/30/under-armour-debuts-made-in-the-u-s-gear-and-tests-what-we-think-we-know-about-manufacturing-in-america/.

Harrington, H. James. 2009. *Fast-Action Solution Technique, Little Big Book Series for Performance Improvement.* Chico, CA: Paton Professional.

Harrington, H. James, and Frank Voehl. 2016a. *The Innovation Tools Handbook: Creative Tools, Methods, and Techniques that Every Innovator Must Know,* vol. 3. Boca Raton, FL: CRC Press/Taylor & Francis Group.

Harrington, H. J., and Brett Trusko. 2014. *Maximizing Value Propositions to Increase Project Success Rates, The Little Big Book Series.* Boca Raton: Productivity Press.

Harrington, H. J., and Frank Voehl. 2020. *The Innovation Systems Cycle: Simplifying and Incorporating the Guidelines of the ISO 56002 Standard and Best Practices, The Little Big Book Series.* Boca Raton, FL: CRC Press/Taylor & Francis Group.

Harrington, H. J., and Frank Voehl. 2016c. *The Innovation Tools Handbook: Organizational and Operational Tools, Methods and Techniques that Every Innovator Must Know,* vol. 1. Boca Raton, FL: CRC Press/Taylor & Francis Group

Harrington, James H., and Frank Voehl. 2016d. *The Innovation Tools Handbook: Evolutionary and Improvement Tools that Every Innovator Must Know.* Boca Raton, FL: CRC Press/ Taylor & Francis Group.

Heidari-Robinson, Stephen, and Suzanne Heywood. 2016. *ReOrg: How to Get It Right.* Boston: Harvard Business Review Press.

Henke, N., A. Puri, and T. Saleh. 2020. "Accelerating Analytics to Navigate COVID-19 and the Next Normal." McKinsey Analytics (May).

holacracy.org. n.d.

Hopkins, Renee. 2016. "7 Best Practices for Business Model Innovation." https://www.linkedin.com/pulse/7-best-practices-business-model-innovation-renee-hopkins/.

Hyken, Shep. 2016. How Effective is Net Promoter Score (NPS)?" (December 3). https://www.forbes.com/sites/shephyken/2016/12/03/how-effective-is-net-promoter-score-nps/#69b41b5623e4.

Innovation Zen. 2006. "The Abernathy – Utterback Model." (August 29). https://innovationzen.com/blog/2006/08/29/innovation-management-theory-part-6/.

ISO 56002:2019. Innovation management—Innovation management system—Guidance. Geneva, Switzerland: ISO copyright office

Jaruzelski, Barry, Robert Chwalik, Brad Goehle, and Bar. 2018. "What the Top Innovators Get Right." https://www.strategy-business.com/feature/What-the-Top-Innovators-Get-Right?gko=bdbc7

Juran, J. M., and Joseph A. De Feo. 2010. *Juran's Quality Handbook: The Complete Guide to Performance Excellence,* 6th edition. New York: McGraw Hill.

Kahneman, Daniel. 2013. *Thinking, Fast and Slow.* New York: Farrar, Straus, and Giroux.

Kapoor, Michael, and Martin Koehring, ed. 2014. "Creating a seamless customer experience." *The Economist.*

Kaushik, Sunil Kumar V. 2017. *Innovative Business Management Using TRIZ.* Milwaukee, WI: ASQ Quality Press.

Keathley, Jane. 2014. *The Executive Guide to Innovation: Turning Good Ideas Into Great Results.* Milwaukee, WI: ASQ Quality Press.

Keathley, Jane. 2015. Is it Innovation or Improvement? ASQ World Conference Proceedings. http://asq.org/innovation-group/2015/10/is-it-innovation-or-improvement.pdf.

Keathley, Jane. 2019. "Knowing When You've Added Value." *Quality Progress* 52, no. 3:16-23.

King, Andrew, and Jeanne Liedtka. 2014. "How Design Thinking Engaged Dubliners in Community Revitalization." *Washington Post.* https://www.washingtonpost.com/business/how-design-thinking-engaged-dubliners-in-community-revitalization/2014/03/21/01fc2ec4-addb-11e3-a49e-76adc9210f19_story.html.

Kotter, John. 2012. "Accelerate!" *Harvard Business Review.*

Kotter, John. 2014a. Reinventing the Company for the Digital Age. Accessed January 21, 2020. https://www.bbvaopenmind.com/wp-content/uploads/2015/02/BBVA-OpenMind-book-Reinventing-the-Company-in-the-Digital-Age-business-innovation1.pdf.

Kotter, John P. 2014b. *Accelerate: Building Strategic Agility for a Faster Moving World.* Boston: Harvard Business Review Press.

Laja, Peep. 2019. "How to Create a Unique Value Proposition (with Examples)." https://cxl.com/blog/value-proposition-examples-how-to-create/.

Larsen, Gabe. 2020. "Inside Sales vs. Outside Sales: How to Structure a Sales Team." Accessed June 3, 2020. https://blog.hubspot.com/sales/inside-vs-outside-sales#:~:text=Furthermore%2C%20sales%20reps%20work%20differently,face%2Dto%2Dface%20sales.

Liedtka, Jeanne, Daisy Azer, and Randy Salzman. 2017. *Design Thinking for the Greater Good: Innovation in the Social Sector.* New York: Columbia Business School Publishing.

Liedtka, Jeanne, Andrew King, and Kevin B. Bennett. 2013. *Solving Problems with Design Thinking: 10 Stories of What Works.* New York: Columbia Business School Publishing.

Liedtka, Jeanne, and Tim Ogilvie. 2011. *Designing for Growth: A Design Thinking Tool Kit for Managers.* New York: Columbia University Press.

Liedtka, Jeanne. 2015. *The Essential Guide to Design Thinking.* Charlottesville, VA: University of Virginia Darden School of Business.

Lindborg, H. J. 2020. "Adapt and Evolve." *Quality Progress* 55, no. 4:28-22.

Lyke-Ho-Gland, Holly. 2016. "Picking Up the Pace." *Quality Digest.*

Maechler, Nicolas, Jonathan Michael, Robert Schiff, and Thomas Rüdiger Smith. 2018. "Managing a Customer-Experience Transformation in Banking." Accessed January 31, 2020. https://www.mckinsey.com/industries/financial-services/our-insights/managing-a-customer-experience-transformation-in-banking.

Markowitz, Jaclyn. 2018. "Open Innovation at Lego – The Back Beat in 'Everything is Awesome'." https://digital.hbs.edu/platform-rctom/submission/open-innovation-at-lego-the-back-beat-in-everything-is-awesome/.

Martin, Roger. 2011. "The Innovation Catalysts." *Harvard Business Review.*

Martin, Steve W. 2013. "The Trend that is Changing Sales." https://hbr.org/2013/11/the-trend-that-is-changing-sales%20 April%2025%202017.

Masters, Kristin, 2017. The Impact of Industry 4.0 on the Automotive Industry. Accessed June 3, 2020. https://blog.flexise.com/the-impact-of-industry-4.0-on-the-automotive-industry.

Maurya, Ash. 2012. *Running Lean: Iterate from Plan A to a Plan That Works,* 2nd edition. Sebastopol, CA: O'Reilly.

McChrystal, Stanley A., Tantum Collins, David Silverman, and Chris Fussell. 2015. *Team of Teams: New Rules of Engagement for a Complex World.* New York: Portfolio/Penguin.

McDowell, Tiffany, Dimple Agarwal, Don Miller, Tsutomu Okamoto, and Trevor Page. 2016. "Organizational Design: The Rise of Teams." Deloitte Insights.

McKinsey Quarterly. 2008. Enduring Ideas: The 7-S Framework, https://www.mckinsey.com/business-functions/strategy-and-corporate-finance/our-insights/enduring-ideas-the-7-s-framework

Merrill, Peter. 2019. "Deep Dive." *Quality Progress* 52, no. 5:56-58.

Meyer, Pauline. 2019a. "Amazon.com Inc.'s Organizational Structure Characteristics (An Analysis)." http://panmore.com/amazon-com-inc-organizational-structure-characteristics-analysis.

Meyer, Pauline. 2019b. "Apple Inc.'s Organizational Structure & Its Characteristics (An Analysis)." (February 15). http://panmore.com/apple-inc-organizational-structure-features-pros-cons.

Meyer, Pauline. 2019c. "Starbucks Coffee Five Forces Analysis (Porter's Model) & Recommendations." http://panmore.com/starbucks-coffee-five-forces-analysis-porters-model.

Meyer, Pauline. 2019d. "Starbucks Coffee's Organizational Structure & Its Characteristics." http://panmore.com/starbucks-coffee-company-organizational-structure.

Miller, Mark J. 2016. "Forrester Customer Experience Index Finds CX Bar Continues to Rise." https://www.brandchannel.com/2016/07/26/forrester-customer-experience-index-072616/.

Mind Tools Content Team. "McKinsey 7-S Framework Making Every Part of Your Organization Work in Harmony."

Mohr, Tom. 2019. "In the Loop — Chapter 23: Starbucks." CEOQuest. (October 8). https://medium.com/ceoquest/in-the-loop-chapter-23-starbucks-771e6cd6a11c.

Nagji, Bansi, and George Tuff. 2012. "Managing Your Innovation Portfolio." *Harvard Business Review* (May).

Neave, Henry R. 1990. *The Deming Dimension.* Knoxville, TN: SPC Press.

Newbold, Curtis. 2018. "How to Do Ethnography Research." Accessed January 23, 2020. https://thevisualcommunicationguy.com/2018/01/30/how-to-do-ethnography-research/.

Ogburn, Charlton Jr. 1957. "Merrill's Marauders." *Harper's Magazine.*

Orgchart. 2019. "Essentials on Managing Reorgs." https://www.orgchartpro.com/essentials-managing-reorgs/.

Osterwalder, Alexander. 2012. "Achieve Product-Market Fit with Our Brand-New Value Proposition Designer." http://businessmodelalchemist.com/blog/2012/08/achieve-product-market-fit-with-our-brand-new-value-proposition-designer.html.

Osterwalder, Alexander, Yves Pigneur, Gregory Bernarda, and Alan Smith. 2014. *Value Proposition Design: How to Create Products and Services Customers Want.* Hoboken, NJ: John Wiley & Sons.

Osterwalder, Alexander, Yves Pigneur, and Tim Clark. 2010. *Business Model Generation: A Handbook for Visionaries, Game Changers, and Challengers.* Hoboken, NJ: John Wiley & Sons.

Poosen, Peter P., and Tatsuya Nakagawa. 2008. "Innovation 101: Whirlpool's Spin on Innovation." (July 14). https://www.industryweek.com/leadership/companies-executives/article/21933039/innovation-101-whirlpools-spin-on-innovation.

Price, Perry. 2019. "Elevating the Customer Experience in Banking." *No Jitter, Contact Center and Customer Experience.* https://www.nojitter.com/contact-center-customer-experience/elevating-customer-experience-banking.

Radziwill, Nicole. n.d. "New Era of Quality: Big Data and Predictive Analytics." ASQ TV.

Rao, Jae, James Wilson, and Jim Watkinson. 2009. "What is Innovation? Part 2: A Web View of How IBM Approaches Innovation." https://innovationatwork.wordpress.com/tag/innovation-at-ibm/.

Reeves, Martin, and J. Fuller. 2020. "We Need Imagination Now More Than Ever." *Harvard Business Review* (April 10).

Reichheld, Frederick F., and Rob Markey. 2011. *The Ultimate Question 2.0: How Net Promoter Companies Thrive in a Customer-Driven World.* Boston: Harvard Business Press.

Ries, Eric. 2011. *The Lean Startup: How Today's Entrepreneurs Use Continuous Innovation to Create Radically Successful Businesses.* New York: Crown Business.

Ries, Eric. 2017. *The Startup Way: How Modern Companies Use Entrepreneurial Management to Transform Culture and Drive Long-Term Growth.* New York: Currency.

Robertson, Brian J. 2015. Holacracy: *The New Management System for a Rapidly Changing World.* New York: Henry Holt and Company, LLC.

Röll, Juliane. 2019. "Who is Using Holacracy? Structure and Process: Organizational Development." http://structureprocess.com/holacracy-cases/.

Samson, Alain. 2014. "An Introduction to Behavioral Economics." https://www.behavioraleconomics.com/the-be-guide/the-behavioral-economics-guide-2014/.

Sangasubana, N. 2009. "How to Conduct Ethnographic Research." *The Qualitative Report* 16:567-573.

Satell, Greg. 2016. "How IBM Innovates." https://www.forbes.com/sites/gregsatell/2016/01/19/how-ibm-innovates/#4de0ccce7f60.

Satell, Greg. 2017. *Mapping Innovation: A Playbook for Navigating a Disruptive Age.* New York: McGraw-Hill.

Satell, Greg. 2018. "How IBM, Google and Amazon Innovate Differently." https://www.inc.com/greg-satell/how-ibm-google-amazon-innovate-differently.html.

Silverman, Craig. 2015. "The Best Practices for Innovation Within News Organizations." https://www.americanpressinstitute.org/publications/reports/strategy-studies/best-practices-for-innovation/single-page/.

Smithson, Nathaniel. 2019. "Google's Organizational Structure & Organizational Culture (An Analysis)." Panmore Institute. http://panmore.com/google-organizational-structure-organizational-culture.

Snee, Ronald D., Richard D. DeVeaux, and Roger W. Hoerl. 2014. "Follow the Fundamentals." *Quality Progress* 47, no. 1:24-28.

Spotio, 2018. The Consultative Selling Approach. https://spotio.com/blog/consultative-selling/

Tague, Nancy R. 2005. *The Quality Toolbox,* 2nd edition. Milwaukee, WI: ASQ Quality Press.

techopedia.com. 2020. "Service Management System (SMS)." techopedia.com. Accessed February 14, 2020. https://www.techopedia.com/definition/30103/service-management-system-sms.

Temkin, Bruce, Moira Dorsey, and David Segall. 2019. ROI of Customer Experience 2019. *In Insight Report.* Provo, UT: Qualtrix XM Institute.

Thompson, Derek. 2014. "Finding the Next Edison." *The Atlantic.*

Thompson, Derek. 2017. "Google's Moonshot Factory." *The Atlantic,* 61-74.

Uphill, Kevin. 2016. *Creating Competitive Advantage: How to Be Strategically Ahead in Changing Markets.* London; Philadelphia: Kogan Page.

Voehl, Christopher F., H. J. Harrington, and William S. Ruggles. 2016. *Effective Portfolio Management Systems.* Boca Raton, FL: CRC Press/Taylor & Francis Group.

Voehl, Frank, and H. J. Harrington. 2016. *Change Management: Manage the Change or It Will Manage You: Management Handbooks for Results Series*. Boca Raton, FL: CRC Press/ Taylor & Francis Group.

Weir, Mike. 2018. "What is a Customer Journey Map and Why Are They Important?" Accessed June 2, 2020. https://business.linkedin.com/ marketing-solutions/blog/sales-and-marketing/2018/customer-journey-map-definition-benefits-examples .

Wells, Marshall, and Kralj, Miha. 2016. "The Case for Automation." (April 29). https://www.accenture.com/us-en/blogs/blogs-case-for-automation.

Womack, James P., and Daniel T. Jones. 2003. *Lean Thinking*. New York: Simon & Schuster Audio.

Tools and Skills for the Innovation Structure

IN THE PAST, ORGANIZATIONS WERE STRUCTURED around the concepts of "plan and control" to achieve consistent outcomes. We have entered the era when these objectives no longer get us where we need to be. Our structural models are overdue for innovative updates to meet the needs of the modern marketplace.

There are many tools, technologies, and skills that can help the organization address its structural gaps and inconsistencies and achieve its desired innovation structure. Without these necessary resources, people will struggle to move forward with new ideas, or they may become complacent, allowing the status quo to rule the day; neither of these situations leads to the cutting-edge developments that innovative organizations are so good at. A few of these tools and skill sets are reviewed in this section:

- Business model canvas
- Decision matrix
- Design for Six Sigma
- Design thinking
- Ethnography
- Fast action solution team (FAST)
- Holacracy
- Innovation maturity
- Innovation portfolio
- Kano
- Knowledge management system (KMS)
- Lean start-up
- Lean Six Sigma
- Net promoter score
- Open innovation
- Open office
- Opportunity centers
- Organization chart

- Organizational network analysis
- Quality function deployment
- Service blueprinting
- Skills for innovation

- TRIZ
- Value analysis
- Value engineering

This is a short list. There are many tools available, and most traditional quality management tools can be applied for innovation. The following references contain more information on innovation tools:

- *The Innovation Tools Handbook, Volume 1: Organizational and Operational Tools, Methods, and Techniques that Every Innovator Must Know* (Harrington and Voehl 2016c)

- *The Innovation Tools Handbook, Volume 2: Evolutionary and Improvement Tools that Every Innovator Must Know* (Harrington and Voehl 2016d)

- *The Innovation Tools Handbook, Volume 3: Creative Tools, Methods, and Techniques that Every Innovator Must Know* (Harrington and Voehl 2016a)

- *The Executive Guide to Innovation, Turning Good Ideas into Great Results* (Keathley 2014)

Tools may be especially useful at different parts of the innovation progression, as shown in Figure B.1. Creativity tools will be most useful early on as potential opportunities and solutions are being identified. Design and rapid development tools will be needed as the solution moves into development, and business model and marketing tools will be most useful as the solution rolls out to users. Tools for objectively capturing user and customers likes and dislikes, while very important early on, should continue to be used through development and deployment; you never know when user needs may change. A simpler, more effective solution than yours may come along, or your supply chain may be disrupted. You always need a plan B to keep customers engaged and happy.

An End-to-End Innovation Process
Adapting the tools honed by startups.

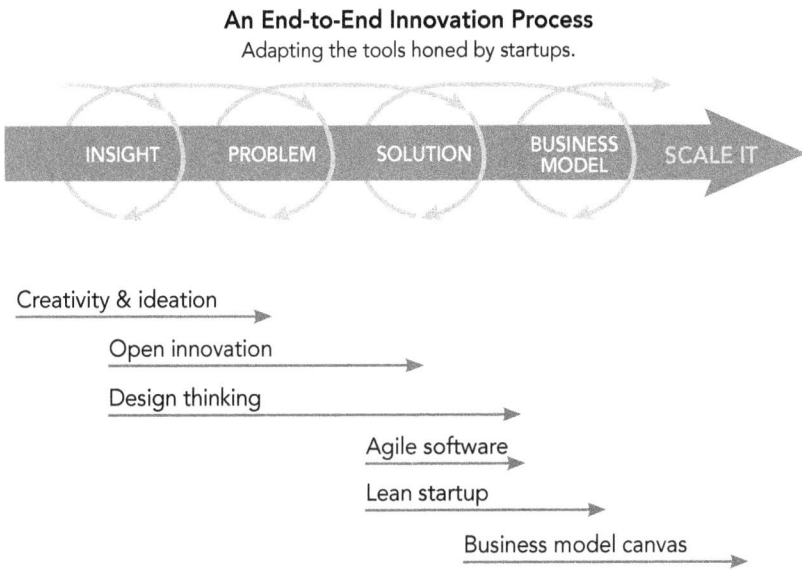

Creativity & ideation

Open innovation

Design thinking

Agile software

Lean startup

Business model canvas

Figure B.1   Applying tools and methodologies by innovation phase.

(Source: Furr and Cyer 2014; used with permission.)

BUSINESS MODEL CANVAS

The business model canvas and the closely related lean canvas are one-page models for succinctly describing a business plan and strategy (see Figure B.2). Using a one-page business model to capture the business plan and strategy is useful for innovation strategies because it clarifies and simplifies the concept and the key elements of moving the concept forward. It avoids the need for a lengthy, detailed business plan.

The business model canvas can be shared easily with team members and other interested parties, serving as a communication tool and discussion basis. It lends itself to online posting and virtual meeting platforms. It can be changed quickly when updates are needed.

Using the lean canvas adaptation, the business plan keeps the focus on the business model for the offering rather than narrowing the focus to the solution. This bigger-picture approach helps ensure success by

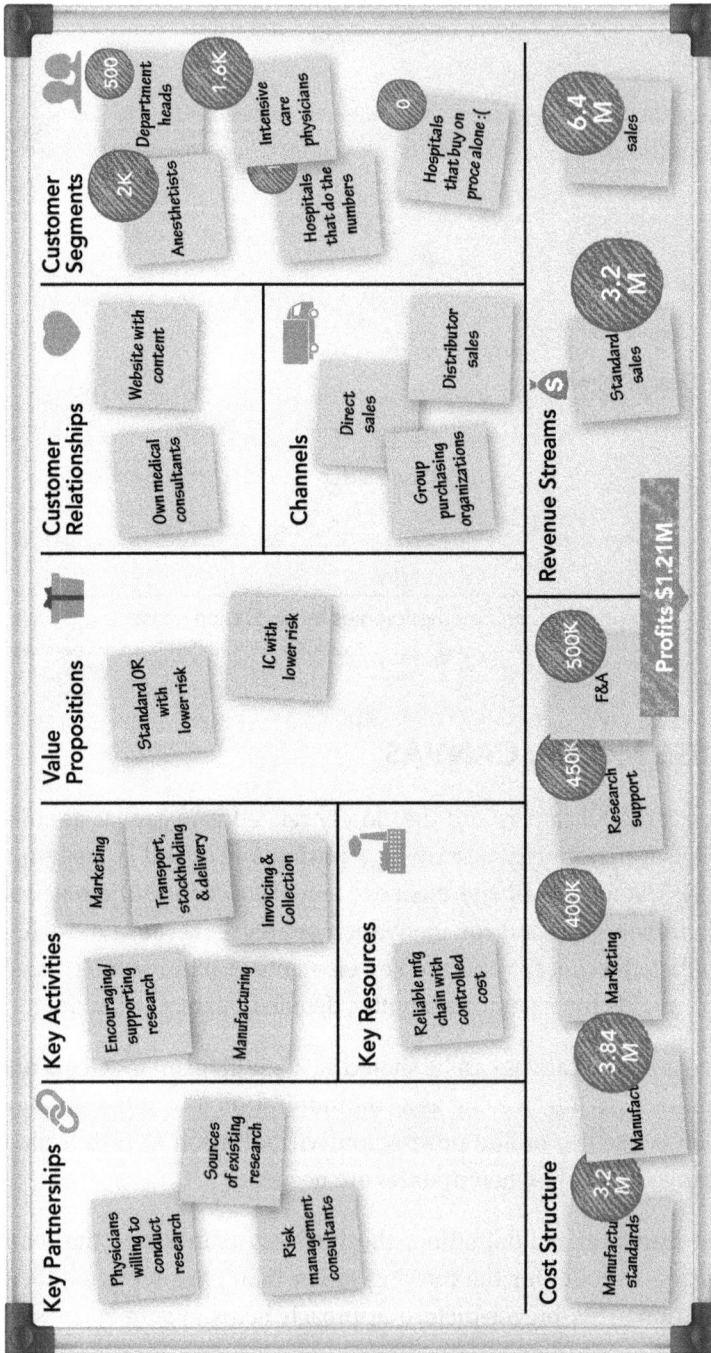

Figure B.2 Example of business model canvas.

(Source: Strategyzer; used with permission.)

considering the customer segments, competition, delivery models, and cost structures throughout the solution development. Risk management and value proposition are inherent in the business model plan (Maurya 2012; Osterwalder, Pigneur, and Clark 2010).

DECISION MATRIX

A decision matrix, also known as Pugh matrix, is a model for weighing issues and prioritizing them for action. It is used to evaluate and prioritize a list of options. The team first establishes a list of weighted criteria and then evaluates each option against those criteria. It is useful when a list of options must be narrowed to one choice, when the decision must be made on the basis of several criteria, or after the list of options has been reduced to a manageable number by list reduction.

The decision matrix can help to shorten a long list of potential problems to solve or solutions to develop. The criteria used often fall under the categories of effectiveness, feasibility, capability, cost, time required, support, or enthusiasm (of team and of others). The matrix is best used to summarize data that have been collected about the various criteria rather than opinions or unsubstantiated options. The rating of the options will only be as good as the assumptions and data on which it is based (Tague 2005).

DESIGN FOR SIX SIGMA

Design for Six Sigma is a methodology that focuses on creative designs for greater process or product/service performance. The methodology defines five steps: define, measure, analyze, design, and verify (DMADV) to follow to achieve continuous innovation. The model uses customer/ user needs to define the initial business case, which outlines the project's key priorities, e.g., user value proposition, acceptable defect rates. Potential solution designs are vetted through a variety of data analyses, using tools such as value analysis, risk analysis, TRIZ, and/or QFD matrices. Through rounds of testing and redesigns, with empirical measures at each step, solutions are developed with innovative features and characteristics that provide the high-quality, value-adding processes, product, services, and business model that move the organization forward (Juran and De Feo 2010).

DESIGN THINKING

Design thinking can be described in four phrases, or key questions, that form the process:

- **Phase I: What is?** — a deep dive into understanding the problem

- **Phase II: What if?** — creating a list of potential solutions

- **Phase III: What wows?** — finding the potential solutions most likely to create value through prototyping and early analyses

- **Phase IV: What works?** — begin to move the solution to the marketplace in small, limited environments

Tools such as journey mapping, storytelling, visualization, and prototyping are used to bring about a better understanding of what the problem is and how it can best be solved. Organizationally, design thinking is a useful tool for the problem characterization and solution selection phases of product development. These functions are typically the responsibility of product or marketing managers or the R&D group, with handoffs to operations when the "What works?" question has been answered (Liedtka 2015; Liedtka and Ogilvie 2011).

ETHNOGRAPHY

Ethnography is the science of understanding human behaviors in their cultural context. Ethnographers observe the day-to-day activities of members of the culture, noting action patterns and practices. It is generally qualitative in nature, based on the non-directed observations of people in their natural environment by trained and experienced researchers. The approach allows a much deeper look at people's behaviors without the distortion of a forced setting, such as a focus group or test lab. Controlling for data quality includes limiting the reactivity of subjects to the data collection process and ensuring the reliability and validity of the data collected (Newbold 2018; Sangasubana 2009; Anderson 2009).

The methodology includes several phases:

- Establish the problem and research questions

- Select the appropriate setting and acquire the necessary permissions and access

- Determine the approach(es) for data collection
  - Observation/participation
  - Interviews
  - Archival data

- Gather and record the data

- Code and analyze the data for patterns, outliers, constructs, and theories

FAST ACTION SOLUTION TEAM (FAST)

In the mid-1990s, a number of organizations, including Ford and General Motors, worked to implement rapid problem-solving methodologies that led to significant savings through process improvements. The name of the activity varied to meet the individual company's preference, e.g., at Ford, it was called "RAPID." These "fast action solution teams (FAST)" were designed to pick low-hanging fruit and find solutions in one to two days, and then implement them in the next 90 days. The methodology could be applied to both processes and subprocesses. Management sponsorship was a requirement for success (Harrington 2009).

The FAST methodology is made up of seven phases; these phases describe a useful problem-solving approach for process innovation:

1. Establish the methodology process

2. Define the immediate opportunities

3. Research potential solutions

4. Define process change improvement

5. Approve individual changes

6. Implement the changes

7. Measure the results

HOLACRACY

One model that does away entirely with hierarchical authorities and traditional structures is holacracy. The holacracy management system was developed by Brian J. Robertson; it is in use at a growing number of corporations including Zappos, Valsplat, and many others (Robertson 2015; Röll 2019; holacracy.org n.d.). The holacracy model introduces transformative new structures for personnel organization and decision-making. Systems are organized around work rather than around people. Holacracy organization charts are structured as groups, or circles, of roles, rather than the traditional tree model, and they change frequently, sometimes multiple times per day, as people join and leave circles. Each circle is a self-organizing entity on its own that is part of a larger circle, which may be part of an even larger circle, up to the largest circle, which is the organization. Executive leadership's role in a holacracy is to enable the conditions that allow its people to thrive, both as individuals and as contributors to the organization.

The holacracy system comprises two functions: governance and operations. Governance is the part of the system in which authorities and expectations are set, based on strict rules and specific formats. Governance covers activities such as creating, amending, and removing roles, policies, and subgroups or (subcircles, as the model calls them). Governance uses an integrative process to gather and evaluate inputs. There is not a single leader but rather someone who fills the role of facilitator. Governance does not deal with execution or operational decisions; these are addressed in day-to-day activities and/or tactical meetings. When done correctly, and given time to become integrated into the organization, good governance reduces wasted time by defining clear accountabilities and expectations, allowing workers to "find their own intrinsic motivation and the autonomy and authority to act on it."

Operations then becomes a well-oiled, efficient execution machine. It includes processes for coordinating teams and their work, including identification of projects, their required activities, and their sequencing and prioritization. Workers are responsible not only for completing the work for their role but also for communications, updates, and requests to other circle members. Tactical meetings may be held but most of the communications occur through informal discussions, shared spaces with visible work information, and specific checklists and metrics. Holacracy operations depend on individual accountability, team transparency, and flexible, fast-paced meetings.

The holacracy management system reflects changes occurring in society, e.g., self-organizing networks, online communities, instant communications, and flexible, adaptable practices. Moving your organization's structure in this direction will be a useful driver for innovation. Anticipate frequent organization changes — write your organizational chart in pencil, as David Burkus writes in *Under New Management* and allow your teams to form and reform as the work demands (see Chapter 9; also Burkus 2016).

INNOVATION MATURITY

Innovation maturity evaluates the life cycle of an innovation for the purpose of pipeline planning and anticipating resource needs. The Abernathy-Utterback model (Innovation Zen 2006; Abernathy and Utterback 1978) evaluates innovation maturity from the early fluid stage, through the transitional phase, to the mature "specific" phase. During the fluid phase, the focus is on addressing the pain point and making rapid changes to adapt the solution to the user's needs and desires. Processes will be chaotic and changing frequently. As the offering matures and stabilizes, it enters the transitional phase in which the attention turns to the processes around the offering. This is when innovations to process efficiency and effectiveness are introduced.

Eventually, the offering and the related processes become standardized, rate of change slows, and changes, if made, are only minor. At this point, the offering is ripe for disruption, and if the organization has not planned for it, this disruption will come from a competitor (e.g., Blockbuster and Netflix).

Monitoring innovation maturity can help keep the innovation pipeline primed, with a balance of fluid offerings progressing forward to replace those mature offerings at the end of their innovation life cycle.

INNOVATION PORTFOLIO

The innovation ambition matrix, from Nagji and Tuff (2012), can be used to guide the development of the innovation portfolio. The matrix is used to evaluate a new offering based on whether it is a new product, enters a new market, or both. The model categorizes offerings into core, adjacent, and transformational. Risk increases with each category. The innovation ambition matrix helps determine your comfort level for each category (risk tolerance), the desired makeup of the pipeline of new offerings, and the balance across portfolio offerings.

KANO

The Kano model of customer satisfaction is a tool to help understand the customer's expectations, what they consider unacceptable, and what delights them. It is based on customer perceptions of the value and necessity of the offering and its features (see Figure B.3). Two aspects of satisfactions are measured: (1) how well the offering's attributes fulfill the requirements (degree of achievement), and (2) how satisfied they are with the offering, from very dissatisfied to very satisfied. The results are interpreted from five categorical perspectives and used to understand how to best meet the customer's needs:

- Must be — features assumed to be satisfactory that are only noticed if they are missing or deficient

- One-dimensional — features that correlate directly between degree of satisfaction and degree of achievement

- Attractive — features that are unexpected but lead to greater satisfaction (non-linear increase)

- Indifferent—features that were not expected and also not used

- Reverse—features that correlate negatively with satisfaction

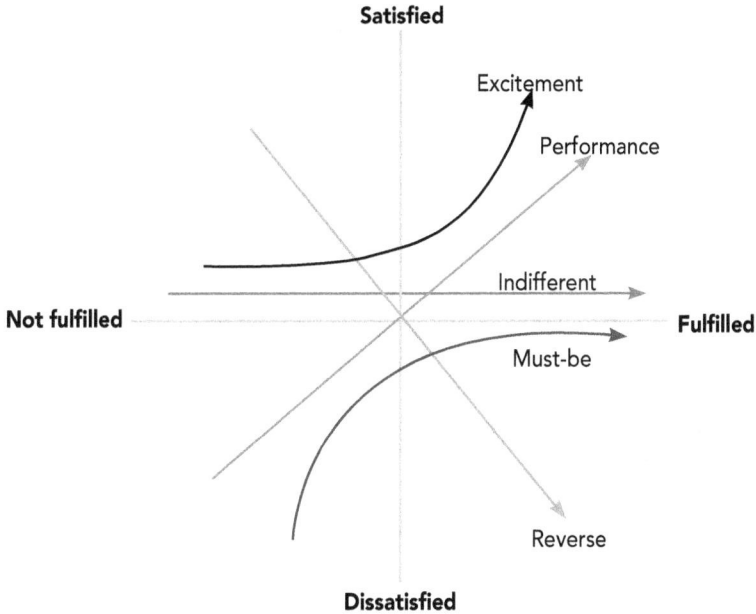

Figure B.3 Kano Model diagram.   (Source: ASQ; used with permission.)

KNOWLEDGE MANAGEMENT SYSTEM

One of the most crucial tools for innovation is an effective KMS. An effective KMS supports both problem-solving and taking advantage of opportunities. It is even effective in helping to recognize potential innovative projects. An effective KMS is a proactive, systematic process by which value is generated from intellectual or knowledge-based assets and disseminated to the stakeholders. Information technology captures both explicit and tacit data.

Explicit (hard) knowledge is knowledge that is stored in a semi-structured content, such as documents, emails, voicemails, or video media. It can be articulated in formal language and readily transmitted to other people.

It is also called hard or tangible knowledge, and it is conveyed from one person to another in a systematic way. Explicit knowledge represents a small percentage of overall organizational knowledge.

Tacit (soft) knowledge is knowledge that is formed around intangible factors embedded in an individual's experience. It often takes the form of beliefs, values, principles, and morals. It guides the individual's actions. It is embedded in the individual's ideas, insights, value, and judgment. It is only accessible through the direct corroboration and communication with the individual who has the knowledge. Tacit knowledge comprises the majority of organizational knowledge and must be factored into the KMS.

It is easy to see why an effective KMS is essential in designing an innovative organizational structure. Care should be taken in designing an organization's system to maximize the accumulation and details related to the organization's intellectual capital.

> *"Already an estimated two thirds of U.S. employees work in the services sector, and "knowledge" is becoming the most important product. This trend calls for different organizations as well as different kinds of workers."*
>
> – Peter Drucker, author and consultant

LEAN START-UP

Lean start-up is a methodology of rapid iterations of design, collection of empiric feedback data, and decisions to achieve a sustainable business model in the least amount of time possible (Ries 2017; Ries 2011). In the LSU model, an idea is first evaluated for its value hypothesis; that is, what problem is being solved and how will this idea creatively resolve it? Using a risk assessment approach, the value hypothesis is characterized by the expected benefits in terms of time saved, dollars realized, and/or user happiness.

The value proposition then forms the basis of empirical experiments to test the hypothesis. These experiments are conducted on a minimum viable product (MVP) — the early version of the product with only the basic, essential functionality. The experiments are designed to test against go/no-go decision criteria. If successful, the development team moves on to the next level of value addition. If not successful, the development team reassesses the value proposition using the new information learned. A new hypothesis is developed, or the solution is tabled and another one is pursued.

The LSU framework minimizes risk by expending only the amount of resources required to get to the next value decision, rapidly progressing along the critical pathway toward successful product launch. Its objective is to systematically remove wasted time and effort in the pursuit of entrepreneurial concept to market-ready product.

Success must be defined prior to the experiment and adhered to once the experimental data are obtained. Do not go back to the same MVP solution with different measures of success until you find one that works. Organizational leaders must be willing to make the tough decisions to end or table a project when called for by objective information. The focus can then remain on what is most feasible or fits best with the overall strategy and portfolio. Relying on vanity metrics (that tell you what you want to hear) will not serve you well in the fast-moving world of innovation.

LEAN AND SIX SIGMA

We've known for a long time that the Six Sigma tool kit, so prominent for organizational problem-solving, can readily be applied for innovation purposes. Initially developed with defect reduction and process optimization in mind, the methodology lends itself for use in the evaluation of new information such as user feedback, process efficiency data, and new product performance to drive innovation activities. In these settings, a higher level of risk will need to be accepted to avoid constraining innovative solutions before their true value proposition is clear (Box and Woodall 2012; Keathley 2014).

Similarly, lean techniques, which were developed to eliminate waste, use customer/user value as the starting point; any process steps or product features that do not add positively to the value proposition are considered waste and are subject to modification or removal. The lean focus on linking changes to improved customer/user value is a key characteristic of innovation. When used in combination, these tool sets are referred to as Lean Six Sigma and provide a powerful methodology that helps organizations maximize value through breakthrough performance in their operations and marketplaces (Juran and De Feo 2010).

NET PROMOTER SCORE

For the NPS, customers (or employees) answer this question: "On a scale of 0 to 10, with 10 being the highest, what is the likelihood that you would recommend us (our company) to a friend or colleague?" Resulting scores fall into three groups: scores of 9 or 10 indicate "promoters," scores of 7 or 8 are in the "passive" group, and scores of 6 or less are "detractors." The NPS is calculated as the percentage of promoters (9s and 10s) minus the percentage of detractors (6s and lower) (Reichheld and Markey 2011). A score above 0 is generally considered acceptable, while a score of 50 is considered excellent and anything above 70 is exceptional. The NPS is used to identify areas where the customer relationship can be strengthened; it is also useful to benchmark your organization against others. The NPS question is often used in combination with more open-ended questions to obtain feedback on the reasons for the responder's score.

ORGANIZATIONAL NETWORK ANALYSIS

Organizational network analysis, or ONA, is defined as a "structured way to visualize how communications, information, and decisions flow through an organization" (see Figure B.4). The model groups people into three categories. There are the connectors, those individuals who gather and share information (central nodes); the experts, who have good contacts outside the organization (knowledge brokers); and the outliers, who are not well connected but hold valuable knowledge or skills that are at risk of being lost to the organization (peripherals).

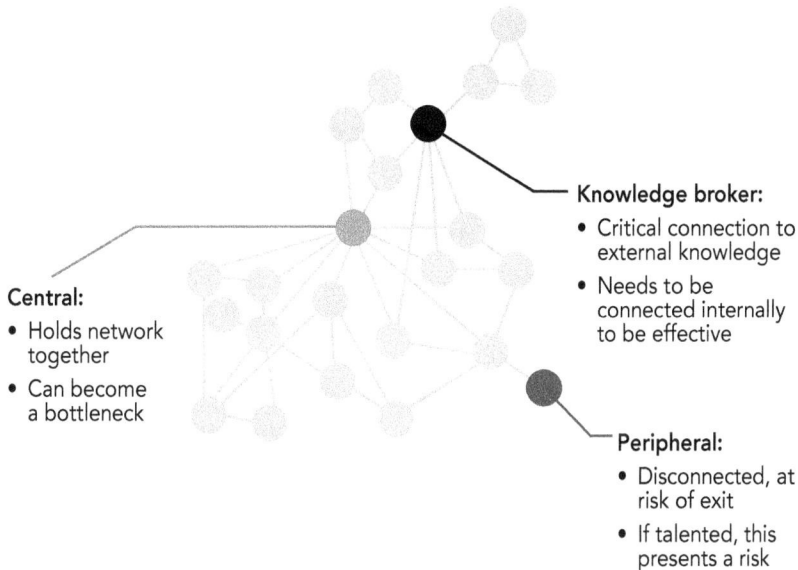

Knowledge broker:
- Critical connection to external knowledge
- Needs to be connected internally to be effective

Central:
- Holds network together
- Can become a bottleneck

Peripheral:
- Disconnected, at risk of exit
- If talented, this presents a risk

Figure B.4 Schematic of the organizational network analysis.

(Source: Deloitte 2016; used with permission.)

Understanding these informal networks, diagraming them, and measuring the relationships and flow of communication can be a useful approach for identifying key communication channels and bottlenecks, missing knowledge and competencies, and at-risk or under-utilized expertise (Bersin 2016).

OPEN INNOVATION

Another change to traditional structures is the concept of "open innovation." Open innovation refers to opening up networks to the outside to take advantage of ideas, resources, and technology from a broader range of sources. Because innovation typically occurs so rapidly, organizations do not have time to develop all the expertise they may need. The need for secrecy is diminished, too; springing the innovation on the marketplace after a confidential and proprietary development period is a good way to let the competition beat you to the market. There is much greater value in sharing information and ideas with other organizations to partner, make quick adaptations and changes, and stay abreast of the current environment.

Open innovation also allows the organization to develop its customer base and marketplace to be ready and excited when the new offering is available. For example, Lego, the well-known building-block company, used open innovation to turn its fortunes around in 2003. It developed processes to build low-cost prototypes of new products and then engaged its customer base to obtain feedback for further development. An online crowd-sourcing platform was launched, which captured hundreds of new ideas and ultimately led to the introduction of new and successful product lines to attract adult users and female users. More recently, Lego has begun using similar techniques to expand its geographical footprint into new areas and also to develop a middle ground of offerings between toys and the digital world, including mobile game apps and audiovisual productions (Markowitz 2018). Open innovation has enabled Lego to continue to its global leadership in the toys industry.

OPEN OFFICE

Open office (physical environment) includes physical structures that encourage worker interactions, chance meetings, idea sharing, and experimentation as well as wall-less office areas, common areas, and walkways designed to intermix people from multiple parts of the organization, and dedicated time and space for contemplation, creativity exercises, and trial-and-error experimentation. Open-office settings encourage innovative thought and help drive a culture in which creativity and innovation thrive.

OPPORTUNITY CENTERS

Ideas are often lost in organizations because individuals have difficulty expressing them in verbal and/or written form. They may feel it's hard to get the idea in front of the individuals who can make a decision due to organizational barriers. Often, they believe management and/or the engineering group will automatically reject the idea because they did not think of it themselves. To offset these obstacles, some organizations have created a model that brings together the tools, technology, and skills needed to drive innovation—a model that can be thought of as the opportunity center.

The opportunity center is the combination of an organization's suggestion program, knowledge management center, and innovation activities. It is usually part of HR. It provides the home where individuals can get their ideas documented and placed in front of the individuals who can make decisions related to implementation of the idea. Sometimes the idea is outside of the organization's mission but has sufficient merit that, through the opportunity center, individuals can access help and support to set up their own company, thereby encouraging individuals to become innovators. The organization may set goals for each employee, from the janitor to the president, to contribute to the opportunity center, e.g., each employee offers a minimum of two suggestions per month. The opportunity center may also provide training and consulting services related to increasing the organization's creativity and innovation.

ORGANIZATION CHART

The organization's structure is really a model of how its work gets done. The work to be done can be thought of in five parts:

- Jobs or tasks to be done

- The authority to do these jobs

- Departmentalization or grouping of jobs

- Managerial controls of the jobs

- Mechanisms for coordination of the jobs

The first four of these normally show up in the organizational chart, while the last is usually described in the organization's policies and procedures.

The organizational chart was introduced by the rail industry in the middle of the 19th century as a way to manage its growing and widely distributed workforce. It was a major innovation in business management and continues to be used extensively in today's organizational management practices. Traditionally, the organizational chart serves to name the organization's jobs (job titles); orient them in relation to each other, both horizontally and vertically (hierarchy); and group them into work units (departments, divisions, etc.) The organizational chart is then used by management to coordinate job tasks and activities, communicate and explain expected alignments among workers, determine reporting and decision-making authorities, and establish a professional development ladder for employees. The organization's policies and procedures spell out the "what" and the "how" of accomplishing the organization's work within the organizational structure.

We are in a transitional phase of organizational management. The traditional organizational chart is less and less effective for today's organizations, where adaptability and flexibility are required to succeed. Traditional models are too restrictive, slow, and costly, and they rarely inspire the people in them to be creative and innovative. In today's environment, the critical needs for agility, speed, and efficiency are driving major changes to organizational structures. These concepts are elegantly described in General Stanley McChrystal's book, *Team of Teams* (McChrystal et al. 2015; see also Chapter 6). His learnings can be applied not only on the battlefield but also in businesses and organizations of any kind.

QUALITY FUNCTION DEPLOYMENT

Quality function deployment (QFD), also known as house of quality, is a problem-solving tool to objectively analyze issues and opportunities and prioritize them for action. It is a structured method for translating customer requirements into appropriate technical requirements for each stage of the development and deployment of the subject topic. QFD focuses on the voice of the customer and the translation of the customer's needs into design targets and value-adding criteria.

QFD is used across sectors and is helpful for innovative product development; business, site, and test planning; and innovation solution generation. It can improve a company's processes, products, or services; quickly produce an outcome; give definition to the design process; help a team stay focused; allow for easy management and peer review of design activities; and provide a basis for refinements and adjustments as more information is learned.

A typical QFD exercise uses a two-part matrix (see Figure B.5):

1. The horizontal part contains customer information. It lists the customer's needs and wants and determines their relative importance. It also lists customer feedback and complaints.

2. The vertical part contains technical information that responds to customer input. It translates customer needs and wants into language that can be measured, examines the relationship between customer and technical requirements, and contains competitive technical data, the targets or goals set by a company to achieve competitiveness.

House of quality template and benefits

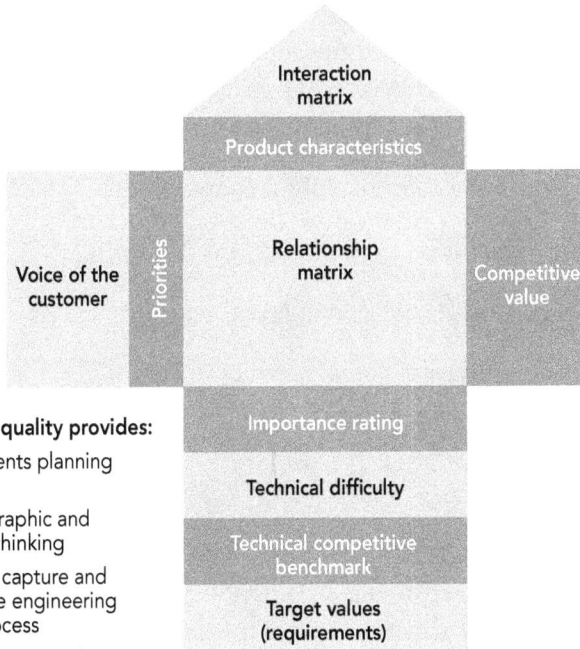

The house of quality provides:

- A requirements planning capability
- A tool for graphic and integrated thinking
- A means to capture and preserve the engineering thought process
- A means to communicate the thought process to new members of the QFD team
- A means to inform management regarding inconsistencies between requirements, risks, and needs of the customer

Figure B.5   Quality function deployment model.

(Source: ASQ; used with permission.)

The target value—the level of performance that needs to be achieved to satisfactorily meet the perceived outcome of an organization's QFD project—is determined by comparing the customers' evaluations to the competitive technical assessments. The corelationships of the technical requirements are then examined. The objective is to locate any requirements that conflict with each other (Keathley 2014).

SERVICE BLUEPRINTING

Service blueprinting is used to define and structure the organization's work from the customer's point of view. This method allows the visualization of the service process from the customer's perspective (see Figure 7.2, Service blueprint model). Underlying support processes are then connected to the customer touchpoints. Service blueprinting puts the customer's impressions and needs first and foremost, helps to develop processes that enhance the customer's experience, and is useful to identify opportunities for innovation in service delivery.

Service blueprinting comprises these components:

- Customer actions

- Onstage/visible contact employee actions

- Backstage/invisible contact employee actions

- Support processes

- Physical evidence

The first step is to clearly define the scope of the service process to be blueprinted and the customer actions, or touchpoints, to the process (e.g., step up to the cash register, log into a website, place a phone call, etc.) From these customer touchpoints, employee actions are established, first the onstage, or face-to-face, interactions, and then the backstage or non-visible actions, such as phone or website contacts, and the tasks needed to prepare for service delivery. Support processes are defined next and include all those activities that do not include direct contact with the customer but are critical to the service delivery, including product supply, resource management, finance, etc. Physical evidence that the customer encounters is also considered because of its ability to influence customer perception and satisfaction (Keathley 2014; Bitner, Ostrom, and Morgan 2008).

SKILLS FOR INNOVATION

Besides tools and technologies, new skills are needed to ensure the structures built for innovation are effective. Managing change with the end goal of optimizing the status quo will not result in the big wins and disruptive changes that are needed for the best innovations. Managers need to focus on coaching and inspiring workers to share their ideas, experiment with them, make mistakes and learn from them, and engage in the organization's goals. As Janice Fraser, noted entrepreneur, says, "Today's world demands a new management approach that transforms the risk of change into an asset" (Eriksson 2017).

One way to help ensure this change is to establish executive-level positions with responsibilities for innovation, e.g., a chief innovation officer (CIO) or chief customer officer (CCO). Do not leave innovation as an add-on management responsibility to be done after all the regular work is finished. Make the organization's focus on innovation highly visible and exciting.

Everyone is creative and can come up with new and unique ideas. The challenge is to select the right kind of people, those who are willing to question the present system and strive to achieve a better system. Other skill sets to develop in these people involve innovation training, coaching, and mentoring. Identify individuals as innovation catalysts, accelerators, or mentors. Make sure they have the skills you desire for the organization, and then set them loose to share those skills throughout the organization.

Entrepreneurial skills are also needed, especially in large organizations. Many big companies are establishing "intrapreneurial" ventures, which are small, dedicated teams that operate as start-ups. They receive funding from internal venture capital groups, much as an independent start-up would, but they have the advantage of leveraging knowledge and resources of the parent company. Whether internal or external, start-up groups possess (or develop) the expertise to identify high-value opportunities, move quickly to creative solutions, and deliver new value to customers and stakeholders; these skills are absolutely critical for innovation and must be accounted for in the organizational structure.

TRIZ

TRIZ is a problem-solving, analysis, and forecasting tool derived from the study of patterns of invention in the global patent literature. The TRIZ methodology was developed by Genrich Altshuller, a Russian inventor, and his colleagues in the mid-20th century. Altshuller and his team researched hundreds of thousands of inventions across many fields and identified patterns and characteristics of the problems addressed by the inventions. TRIZ is used for problem-solving, failure analysis, and systems analysis, and can be applied to creation and improvement of products, services, and systems. One of the key findings of their research is that innovative solutions typically involve information from outside the field in which they were developed.

The TRIZ matrix is a database of known solutions (principles) able to overcome contradictions. For example, you need a static object to be longer without becoming heavier. This is a contradiction. The improving feature is "#4, length of stationary object" and the worsening factor is "#2, weight of stationary object." The TRIZ matrix can be used to discover possible ways to resolve the contradiction, i.e., the principles. The TRIZ matrix can be applied for any type of process or problem (Kaushik 2017; Keathley 2014).

VALUE ANALYSIS

Measuring value is a key component of understanding innovation potential and effectively managing the innovation process. Successful organizations are adept at advancing innovative solutions using value analyses. Knowledge and expertise in performance improvement and problem-solving are directly applicable for value analysis.

As with any useful metric, collecting and analyzing key data provides an objective basis for decisions, such as when to move forward with a creative solution or when to redesign or revise it. In a broader sense, well-thought-out measurements can play a significant role in managing the high levels of uncertainty inherent in innovation. You must be realistic about the level of uncertainty you are dealing with, and you must understand it in empiric terms if you want to reduce it enough to add real value (see Table 4.1, Benefits of measuring value).

One way measuring value can help is to objectively understand the user's problem or need and the feasibility of solving it. Measurements of value can help us understand where value is lacking or missing so we can identify pain points and opportunities for innovation.

For example, in a challenging situation such as getting school children from the drop-off point to their classrooms each morning in an orderly fashion, a value assessment of each activity from "drop-off" to "in their seats" will yield insights into the lowest value activities: Those activities that—if modified—could add the most value to the process. Perhaps it's the way the students are initially greeted, the route taken to their classrooms, or the way their backpacks and coats are handled. Value analysis, perhaps using a value stream or business process map, can help identify the key points at which things break down. These are the best opportunities for innovating and adding value.

When devising innovative solutions, just as with any problem-solving challenge, it is good to have multiple choices. As information and data about these multiple solutions are gathered, value analysis can help compare them and narrow the list to those with the best value proposition, which can be further developed.

Assessing the value of each change is needed to ensure you continue to create and enhance value as the solution is refined, not detract from it by errantly veering away from or overdeveloping the planned value. Users like simplicity and dislike complexity.

For higher-level decisions—such as strategic directions, program portfolios, and supplier relationships—value analysis helps set direction and align organizational initiatives around those that will provide the greatest innovative benefit (Keathley 2019).

VALUE ENGINEERING

Value engineering is the field of engineering that identifies and selects the best value alternatives for designs, materials, processes, and systems. It is described as the science of distinguishing between incurred costs and inherent costs and minimizing those inherent costs. Engineers ask, "Can the cost of this item or step be reduced or eliminated without diminishing the effectiveness, quality, or customer satisfaction?" They ask it repeatedly in iterative cycles, using highly sophisticated algorithms, simulations, and statistical analyses to measure and analyze these questions, in pursuit of the greatest value (Keathley 2019).

Value engineering may be done using the "willingness to pay" (WTP) model, in which value is assessed by determining an individual's WTP for an offering. A common example of WTP is art buying. Value is generally determined by how much the piece will bring in at an art auction. WTP may be determined by offering an alternative. For example, you could spend $10,000 for a new deck on your house. Or, you could spend $100,000 for a three-season room with innovative climate control options (for example, dynamic glass windows that automatically control lighting and temperature). What you are willing to pay is a measurement of the value of the options to you. Do you want budget, excellent, or luxury value?

A more specific type of WTP is the "value of statistical life." This model measures value based on how much an individual is willing to pay for a reduction in the risk of his or her own death. For example, how much will you pay for certain safety features on your car that will reduce your chance of death by X%? The more you would pay, the higher the value. This type of measurement introduces the idea of odds or chances. Value measurements rely on probabilities to improve accuracy.

As data analytics, artificial intelligence, and machine learning become more established in organizations, value engineers across industries are utilizing them to generate more accurate and reliable value predictions and prescriptive decisions for a wide range of the organization's functions, e.g., content management, business intelligence, and customer behaviors.

Index

Note: Numbers followed by *f* and *t* indicate figures and tables.

D

data analytics, 98–99, *101t*
Davenport, Tom, 48
decentralized organization
    customer structure, 33–36
    decision considerations, 28–29
    geographic structure, 29–31
    overview, 27
    product structure, 31–33
decentralized structures, 15, *17t–18t*
decision-making models, 68, 131
decision matrix, 161
decision matrix tool, 97
Deloitte Human Capital Trends 2016
    study, 63, 112
Deming, W. Edwards, 84–85, 92
depression treatment example,
    111–112
design for Six Sigma, 161–162
design perspective, 5–10
design phases, 13
design thinking, 77–79, 96, 162
disruptive innovation, 83–85
distribution channels, multiple, 38
divergence, 32
diversification, product/service,
    31–32
diversity, management of, 23–24
division of labor, 41
Donaville, Rodney, 55
Drucker, Peter, 168
dual operating system model,
    60–62, *61f*
Dublin, Ireland, example, 78–79
duplication of effort/resources, 33
Dyer, Jeff, 111–112
    The Innovator's Method, 68

E

economies of scale, 22, 33
The Economist poll, 53–54
education and training, 48
electronic customer relationships
    management (eCRM), 128
emotional decision-making, 129–131,
    130t

emotional satisfaction, 130–131
employee–customer relationship,
    129–133
engineering model, 58
environmental stability, 28
ethnography, 79–80, 162–163
experience perceptions, 129–131, *130t*
expert acceleration sessions, 92
expertise, as corporate asset, 42–43
explicit knowledge, 167–168
external environment factors, 28

F

FAST (fast action solution teams),
    163–164
Fleming, J.H., 129, 130
fluid phase, 165
Ford Motor Company, 104
Forrester customer experience
    index, 121
Four Prongs of Quality model, 84, *85f*
Fraser, Janice, 177
friction barriers, 12
front-back hybrid structure, 36–40
fully integrated model, 59–60
functional structures, 15, *16t*, 20–26,
    113
functional walls, 12
Furr, Nathan, 111–112
    The Innovator's Method, 68

G

gain creators, 73, *73f*
geographic structure, 29–31
Global Innovation 1000, 87–88
governance and operations, 164–165
grouping options, 7–9, *8t*

H

hard knowledge, 167–168
Harrington, H. James, 11, 15, 119
Hewlett-Packard example, 39–40
hierarchical structures, 24, 68, 137
hierarchy-free model, 62–63
holacracy, 164–165

P

pain points, understanding, 71–72, 82
pain relievers, 73, *73f*
peer-to-peer model, 63
performance management, 48
Pollard, William, 104
power relationships, 4
price concessions, 39
problem-solving tools, 132–133
process improvement upgrades, 96
process innovation
  agile organizations and, 99–102
  characteristics of, 87–88
  data analytics and, 98–99
  design thinking for, 96
  Global Innovation 1000, 87–88
  innovation methodology, 89–92, *90f*
  innovation process, *90f*, 105
  key business processes, 94–95
  methodology, 89–92, *90f*
  process improvement upgrades, 96
  quality system catalyst for, 92–93
  risk tolerance, 97
  structural reorganization for, 141–142
  sustainability and, 104–105
  technology, 102–104
  workforce organization, 93–94
product change management, 80–85, *81t*
product development cycle, 32
product excellence, 32
product focus, 38
product innovation
  customer needs and added value, 73–80, *73f*
  overview, 71–72
  product change management, 80–85
  structural reorganization for, 140–141
product life-cycle management, 82–83
product management model, 57–58
product–market fit, 73–74, *73f*

product structure, 31–33, 32–33
Pugh matrix, 161

Q

quality function deployment (QFD), 174–176, *175f*
quality professionals, 132–133
quality system, for process innovation, 92–93
questioning skills, 74

R

RAPID methodology, 163
rational satisfaction, 130–131
relationships, customer, 35
remote sales, 116–117, *116f*
repeat business, 35
research and development (R&D) expenditures, 87–88
research and development (R&D) model, 56–57
resistance barriers, 12
resource allocation, 4, 38–39, 55
rewards and incentives, 112
Ries, Eric
  The Lean Startup, 74
risk and failure, innovation and, 54, 83
risk-based thinking, 92
risk tolerance, 97
Robertson, Brian J., 164

S

sales and marketing
  definitions, 108
  innovation and, 107–111
  network teams, 113–117, *117f*
  organizational charts, 112–113
  structuring for, 108–110, *109f*
  on the team, 117–118
sales and marketing models, 57, 116–117, *116f*
Samson, Alain, 131–132

About the Authors

JANE KEATHLEY, MS, PMP, helps organizations integrate their quality and innovation management systems. Her professional career spans medical device software development, clinical research, biopharma manufacturing, and diagnostic microbiology. As principal consultant with Keathley and Company, Ms. Keathley provides services to regulated organizations in healthcare-related industries, including start-up companies, focusing on developing innovative products and services while maintaining effective and compliant operations.

Ms. Keathley is a member of the ASQ Board of Directors, served as chair of the Innovation Division, and has served in multiple member leader roles at ASQ. She previously served as a member of the board of directors for the Virginia Senate Productivity and Quality Award (SPQA) program, where she was also the director of examiner training. She served as an examiner for the National Baldrige Performance Excellence Program and for SPQA.

Ms. Keathley holds a master's degree in medical microbiology from Creighton University and a bachelor's degree in medical technology from Wayne State College. She has published and presented widely in quality and other forums. She is a certified project management professional. She can be reached at jkeathley@keathleyandcompany.com.

DR. H. JAMES HARRINGTON is one of the world's quality system gurus with more than 60 years of experience. In the book, *Tech Trending*, Dr. Harrington was referred to as "the quintessential tech trender." *The New York Times* referred to him as having a "...knack for synthesis and an open mind about packaging his knowledge and experience in new ways— characteristics that may matter more as prerequisites for new-economy success than technical wizardry...." He has been involved in developing quality management systems in Europe, South America, North America, the Middle East, Africa, and Asia.

William Clinton, former President of the United States, appointed Dr. Harrington to serve as an ambassador of goodwill.

Dr. Harrington serves as the chief executive officer (CEO) for Harrington Management Systems. He also serves as the chairman of the board for a number of businesses and as the U.S. chairman of chair on technologies for project management at the University of Quebec in Montreal. Dr. Harrington is recognized as one of the world's leaders in applying performance improvement methodologies to business processes. Previously, Dr. Harrington spent 40 years with IBM, mostly in management positions, and 10 years as a principal of Ernst & Young with the title of international quality advisor.

Dr. Harrington's contributions to performance improvement around the world have brought him many honors and awards, including the Edwards Medal, the Lancaster Medal, ASQ's Distinguished Service Medal, and many others. Dr. Harrington was presented with three lifetime achievement awards – one for the work he did in the Middle East, one by APQO, and one by the Abu Dhabi Chamber of Commerce.

Dr. Harrington is an honorary member of ASQ and the International Association for Quality. He was appointed the honorary advisor to the China Quality Control Association, and he was elected to the Singapore Productivity Hall of Fame in 1990. He has been named lifetime honorary president of the Asia Pacific Quality Organization and honorary director of the Association Chilean de Control de Calidad.

Dr. Harrington was elected a Fellow of the British Quality Control Organization and the American Society for Quality (ASQ). He was also elected an honorary member of the quality societies in Taiwan, Argentina, Brazil, Colombia, and Singapore. He is also listed in the "Who's—Who Worldwide" and "Men of Distinction Worldwide." He has presented hundreds of papers on performance improvement and organizational management structure at the local, state, national, and international levels.

Dr. Harrington is a prolific author, publishing hundreds of technical reports and magazine articles. He has authored or co-authored more than 55 books and 10 software packages. His email address is hjh@svinet.com. He prides himself not on the classes he attended, but on what he was able to accomplish with the innovation he has. He served as CEO of three organizations that were all bought out by larger organizations.

NOTES

NOTES

NOTES

NOTES

NOTES

NOTES

NOTES

www.ingramcontent.com/pod-product-compliance
Lightning Source LLC
Chambersburg PA
CBHW031437210326
41599CB00047B/5591